W9-BMM-763

Digital Photography
Pocket Guide

Also available from O'Reilly:

Digital Video Pocket Guide

SECOND EDITION

Digital Photography
Pocket Guide

Derrick Story

O'REILLY®

BEIJING • CAMBRIDGE • FARNHAM • KÖLN
PARIS • SEBASTOPOL • TAIPEI • TOKYO

Digital Photography Pocket Guide, Second Edition
by Derrick Story

Copyright © 2004, 2003 O'Reilly Media, Inc. All rights reserved.
Printed in the United States of America.

Published by O'Reilly Media, Inc., 1005 Gravenstein Highway North,
Sebastopol, CA 95472.

O'Reilly Media, Inc. books may be purchased for educational, business,
or sales promotional use. Online editions are also available for most titles
(*safari.oreilly.com*). For more information, contact our corporate/institu-
tional sales department: 800-998-9938 or *corporate@oreilly.com*.

Editor:	Robert Eckstein
Production Editor:	Philip Dangler
Cover Designer:	Emma Colby
Interior Designers:	David Futato and Melanie Wang
Photographer:	Derrick Story

Print History:

July 2003:	First Edition.
November 2003:	Second Edition.

The O'Reilly logo is a registered trademark of O'Reilly Media, Inc. The
O'Reilly Digital Studio series designations, *Digital Photography Pocket Guide*,
the image of leaves, and related trade dress are trademarks of O'Reilly Media,
Inc.

Many of the designations used by manufacturers and sellers to distinguish
their products are claimed as trademarks. Where those designations appear
in this book, and O'Reilly Media, Inc. was aware of a trademark claim, the
designations have been printed in caps or initial caps.

While every precaution has been taken in the preparation of this book, the
publisher and author assume no responsibility for errors or omissions, or for
damages resulting from the use of the information contained herein.

0-596-00627-6
[DS]

This book is dedicated to Galen Rowell,
who achieved critical acclaim shooting landscape
photography with a 35mm camera.

By doing so, he opened museum and gallery doors to
all small format and digital photographers who want to
display the timeless beauty of nature, but prefer to use
modern tools instead of traditional large format cameras.
Galen and his wife Barbara died in a plane crash on
August 11, 2002 in Inyo County, California.

Contents

Who's in Charge?

When you first pick up a digital camera and hold it in your hands, many thoughts go through your head. Initially, you might wonder where the power button is, or how to turn on the LCD monitor.

Soon, you reach a crossroads with two options before you. The first is to take what you've learned about your camera in the first few minutes, and use that knowledge to take the best pictures you can. Down this path, the camera is merely an acquaintance. It is in charge and does the best it can to help you capture snapshots on vacation or at birthday parties. In return, you try not to drop it and maybe even occasionally clean its lens.

The other path is much different. The first few steps are the steps that everyone takes with a new camera. "How do I make the lens zoom?" "Where's the battery compartment?" But after a short while, you find yourself in territories previously unknown. You begin to wonder, "How can I take a close-up of that flower?" or "Can I shoot a portrait at twilight?"

This book is a friendly guide for those who want to take the second path. Down this road, you and your camera will become close friends. You'll get to know each feature and how it can help you make outstanding images. In a sense, your camera will become an extension of your vision. And that means you're the one making the decisions, not the camera.

How This Book is Organized

Chapter 1: *What Is It?*

> The adventure begins like preparations for any vacation. You have to account for everything that's going to accompany you and know where it is. In Chapter 1, you'll learn every nook and cranny on your camera. Or, if you haven't purchased one yet, you'll discover the features you need and—just as important—the ones you don't.

> Keep your owner's manual handy when you first review Chapter 1. It will help you find where the flash control button is located on your particular model, for instance. Once you find it, this book will show you how to use the different flash modes to take the pictures you want, not the ones the camera dictates.

> Think of Chapter 1 as a detailed map. It tells you where things are and a little about what they do. It's designed for quick reference—answers while on the road. So make sure you keep this book with you. It's designed to fit easily in your camera bag or your back pocket.

Chapter 2: *What Does It Do?*

> By now, you've located the flash button on your camera, and you've even read about the different modes available, such as *fill flash* and *slow synchro*. Terrific. Now when do you use fill flash? What is slow synchro good for?

> Chapter 2 will help you answer those questions. By this time, you're well on your way to becoming close friends with your camera. And you might not notice it, but you've taken control of the situation. In the beginning, the camera made all the decisions. Most of the time they were adequate. Now you're in charge, and your pictures are much better as a result.

Chapter 3: *How Do I…*

> Here you learn more than a dozen important camera techniques. How do you take great outdoor portraits? How can you shoot architecture like a pro? Can you take action shots with a consumer digital camera? Chapter 3 is like an ongoing conversation between two old fishing partners.

> By the time you've experimented with the techniques outlined in this pocket reference, you'll have journeyed well beyond others who chose the first path. Soon you'll begin to visualize how the pictures should look in you mind, then be able to make the camera capture those images so you can share them with others. Isn't that what photography is all about—showing others the world as you see it?

The difference between these two paths is *control*. So, who's in charge: you, or the camera?

What Is It?

Camera makers have packed lots of capability into today's digital models. The camera that you have in your hands, or the one that you're considering buying, probably has more picture-taking ability than you realize. The trick is: how do you discover that hidden potential?

The first steps are to become familiar with your camera's components, then to learn exactly what they do. This chapter explains important features and sets you on the path to mastering your digital camera.

This section looks at the components on the front, back, top, and sides of the camera. Once you're familiar with the external physical buttons and dials, you'll also learn about some of the vital internal parts, such as the image sensor and metering system.

If you're just getting started with digital photography, this information can also help you pick the right model. Each component is rated at one of three levels: *basic*, *intermediate*, or *advanced*. Make a list of the features that best suit your level of photographic experience, then use that list to help you shop. Here's a brief explanation of how each feature is rated in this chapter.

Basic features ❸. These features should be on any digital camera you consider. Avoid a camera that doesn't include all of these components, because odds are you'll be disappointed with its performance.

Intermediate features ❶. In addition to the basics, these features are useful if you have previous photography experience or plan to advance your skill level.

Advanced features ❹. These features are for experienced photographers who are looking for a versatile camera that is capable of producing quality images under a variety of lighting conditions.

If you're most interested in a dependable point-and-shoot camera that costs $300 or less, make sure the models you're considering include all the basic features in this section. Mid-level cameras usually run between $300 and $500 and should include most of the intermediate components; more advanced consumer models that run between $500 and $1,500 should have just about every item listed in this section.

Once you buy your digital camera, or *digicam*, spend some time with the owner's manual to become familiar with its unique design and how to use its controls. After that, keep this guide in your camera bag—not only does it provide a quick reference for the major components, but it will also help you understand how to use those features to take better pictures.

Front of the Camera

Figure 1-1 shows the components on the front of an intermediate-level camera. Notice that the intermediate features include an optical viewfinder, focus assist light, and a microphone port.

Here's a summary of the features that are often located on the front of the camera:

Figure 1-1. The front of an intermediate-level camera.

Flash ❸. Provides additional light for pictures indoors, at
    night, or for outdoor portraits.

Focus assist light ❶. Helps your camera focus in dim light-
    ing by projecting a white beam, or a subtle pattern, onto
    the subject. This light may also shine during red-eye
    reduction flash mode and serve as the warning light
    when the self-timer is activated.

Infrared sensor ❹. Primarily used to communicate with
    the remote control release for cameras that have that
    capability.

Optical viewfinder lens ❶. Enables you to compose the
    picture by looking through the viewfinder lens instead
    of viewing the LCD monitor on the back of the camera.
    Using the optical viewfinder saves battery power, but it
    isn't quite as accurate as the LCD when framing precise
    compositions or close-ups.

Microphone port ❶. Tiny opening on the front, top, or side of
    the camera used to record audio annotations and to add

sound to movie clips. Some cameras that have a *movie mode* might have a microphone, but not all do.

Picture-taking lens ❸ ❶ ❹. Projects the image you're shooting onto the electronic sensor where the picture is recorded. This lens also captures the image you see on the LCD monitor on the back of the camera.

Most cameras list a series of numbers on the barrel of the lens or on the body near it. The first set is usually followed by "mm" (millimeter) and looks something like this:

  5.4–10.8mm or *7–21mm*

These numbers represent the *zooming range* of your lens. Most consumer digital cameras have a zooming range of at least 2x or 3x. A 3x zoom lens typically has a more powerful telephoto (to bring the action closer) than a 2x zoom.

A 5.4–10.8mm lens is called a *2x zoom* (multiply 5.4 times two), and a 7–21mm lens is a *3x zoom*. Basic consumer models with

---

PRO TIP

There is no magic formula you can always apply to translate digital focal lengths to traditional 35mm numbers because the relationship is determined by the size of the camera's sensor. Camera manufacturers will usually tell you what the 35mm equivalent is. Sometimes, as with digital bodies that accept 35mm lenses, they will tell you the size of the sensor and its relationship to your existing lenses. The Canon 10D, for example, has a sensor that's smaller than 35mm film. The result is a focal length factor of 1.6x. So your standard 50mm lens becomes a 80mm telephoto when attached to the Canon 10D. A general rule of thumb is that there's a 50 percent increase from film to digital: a 14mm nominal focal length lens is around a 21mm on a digital SLR. The exceptions are high-end models such as the Canon EOS 1Ds, which have a "full size" sensor— meaning that the lens focal lengths remain the same as in 35mm photography.

a fixed focal length lens (no zoom) will have a single number, such as 7mm.

If you're familiar with 35mm photography, you can translate those digital camera focal lengths into terms that are easier to understand. A 7–21mm zoom lens in the digital world is the rough equivalent of a 35–105mm lens on your traditional SLR.

The second series of numbers usually looks something like this:

1:2.8–4.0 or *1:2.0–2.5*

These numbers represent the *maximum aperture* of the lens at the wide-angle and telephoto setting. Aperture determines the amount of light that can pass through the lens to the camera sensor. Wide apertures, such as 1.8 or 2.0, allow a lot of light to pass through the lens, and are therefore better in low-light conditions. Narrower apertures, such as 5.6 or 8, allow less light through the lens and are less desirable for low-light shooting.

PRO TIP

Lens Ratings

Basic ❸. Single focal length lens, such as 7mm, with a narrow maximum aperture such as 4 or 5.6.

Intermediate ❶. Short zoom lens (2x) with a maximum aperture of 2.8 or 4.

Advanced ❹. Longer zoom lens (3x or longer) with a maximum aperture of 2.0 or 2.5.

Back of the Camera

Figure 1-2 shows the back panel of an intermediate-level, compact camera. Most of the important functions are accessible via buttons below and to the right of the LCD monitor. This

Figure 1-2. Back panel of an intermediate-level compact camera.

is an important design feature to consider when choosing a digicam, because buttons and dials allow you to make quick camera adjustments—faster than scrolling through menus on the LCD monitor.

Common back-panel components include:

Confirmation light ❸. Shines when the camera is focused and ready to fire, or when the flash is ready. Blinking indicator lights usually suggest that you need to make an adjustment before taking the picture.

Diopter adjustment ❶. Allows for manual adjustment of the optical viewfinder to best suit your vision. This feature is usually included only on more advanced cameras.

Display on/off button ❷. Enables you to turn off the display to conserve battery power. This button often has a third option that provides for the display of camera data on the screen while composing the picture. You can typically cycle through these different settings by pushing the button repeatedly.

LCD monitor ❸. Allows for precise framing of the subject, as the image is captured directly through the picture-taking lens. You should always use the LCD monitor in macro mode (for close-ups) or when using the digital zoom function. The LCD monitor is also used for reviewing pictures you've already captured. Most LCD monitors, however, aren't effective in direct sunlight. The image is hard to see. If you shoot lots of outdoor pictures, make sure you have an optical viewfinder as well.

Menu button ❻. Activates the on-screen menu that enables you to set the various functions of the camera. Most likely, you'll use the multifunctional jog dial to navigate through those menus.

Mode dial ❺. Allows you to select various picture-taking and picture-reviewing modes.

Multifunctional jog dial ❶. Allows you to navigate through on-screen menus by pressing the four directional buttons. Sometimes jog dial buttons have two sets of functions: one set for changing settings while in picture-taking mode, and the other for making adjustments in picture-viewing mode. Look for little icons next to the jog dial buttons. They usually represent the functions associated with those buttons in picture-taking mode.

Optical viewfinder ❶. Lets you compose the picture by looking through a separate viewfinder lens instead of the LCD monitor on the back of the camera. Using the optical viewfinder saves battery power, but it isn't quite as accurate for framing precise compositions or close-ups. The optical viewfinder is very useful when shooting outdoors in direct sunlight, because LCD monitors don't fare well under these conditions and are difficult to see.

Set or confirmation button ❻. Press this to confirm a choice. Most cameras insist that you confirm all selections before enabling them. This button is particularly important when erasing pictures, as it makes it impossible to delete a picture by inadvertently pressing the erase button.

Trash button ❽. Removes the current picture displayed on the LCD monitor. This button doesn't usually remove all pictures on a memory card; you have to select the "erase all" function via the onscreen menu.

Top of the Camera

The top deck design of digital cameras can vary widely depending on their features. The Olympus camera illustrated in Figure 1-3, for example, is an advanced amateur/pro model that provides an LCD information screen, mode dial, hot shoe, and button controls on both the top deck and back panel of the camera. Also notice that the LCD monitor swings upward, which offers more flexibility when framing the picture.

Figure 1-3. The top deck of an advanced amateur camera.

Features located on the top of a camera may include:

Hot shoe ❹. Provides a connection for external flash and other camera accessories. The metal contacts allow the camera to communicate with the flash to provide advanced features such as dedicated exposure control.

LCD information screen ❹. Displays camera information, such as number of pictures remaining on the memory card, exposure compensation setting, and flash mode. This screen is particularly handy when you're using the optical viewfinder to compose your pictures with the LCD monitor turned off. Most advanced cameras include an LCD information screen on the top deck.

Mode dial ❹. Allows you to select the picture-taking mode, such as programmed exposure, aperture priority, or manual.

Shutter button ❸. Trips the shutter and also provides focus and exposure lock. For the best pictures, press lightly on the shutter button and hold it in the halfway position to lock the focus and exposure. Once the confirmation light comes on, you're ready to take the picture. Add more pressure until the shutter trips. The trick is not to let up on the shutter button once the focus is locked, but to keep the pressure on in the halfway position until the exposure is made. Almost all digital cameras use this type of two-step shutter button.

Zoom/magnify lever ❶. Use this lever to zoom in and out when composing your image in picture-taking mode. When in picture-review mode, this lever also allows you to magnify your image on the LCD monitor for closer inspection.

Bottom and Sides of the Camera

Memory cards typically load from the side of the camera, while batteries load from the bottom. You'll also see ports to connect your camera to computers and televisions. One tip is to find the matching cords for these ports, test them, and then label each cord so you can easily grab the right one when it's time to go to work.

Camera strap ❸. Secures the camera by allowing you to place a strap around your wrist or neck. Most compact cameras use the wrist-style strap.

Computer connection ❸. Used for transferring pictures from camera to computer. Most cameras provide a Universal Serial Bus (USB) cable to make this connection. Some advanced Single Lens Reflex (SLR) models also provide a faster "FireWire" connection. If you're considering buying a camera with this connector, make sure that your computer is FireWire enabled.

Remote release ❹. Provides firing of camera from distances up to 15 feet. Some remote releases also allow you to operate the zoom lens. For best results, point the sensor on the remote release at the infrared sensor on the front of the camera.

Speaker port ❹. Emits audio playback of digital video or verbal annotations—designed primarily for quick review on location. For best listening quality, upload the data to your computer and use its sound system for playback.

Tripod socket ❸. Attaches the camera to a tripod or flash bracket. Metal sockets are more durable and therefore superior to plastic ones.

Inside the Camera

In this section you'll learn the common features of the innards of digital cameras, starting with how the unit is powered. Figure 1-4 shows the inside of a typical digital camera.

Figure 1-4. The inside of a digital camera is more a world of electronics than of traditional springs, levers, and gears.

Battery

The battery provides the power for camera functions. This is one feature that every digital camera must have. Common battery types are alkaline (for emergency only), lithium-ion, and nickel-metal hydride—the latter two are rechargeable.

If your camera came with alkaline AA batteries, use them for testing, then replace them as soon as possible with rechargeable nickel-metal hydride (NiMH) batteries, which last much longer than alkalines and will save you lots of money over time. It's always good, however, to keep a fresh set of alkalines handy in case your NiMHs run out of juice while you're away from your charger. Another good practice is to have two sets of the rechargeables, so one's always ready to use—they're a little expensive at first, but it's much cheaper than buying new alkalines over and over.

Lithium-ions are very popular with major camera makers such as Sony, Nikon, and Canon. Most of these cameras come with their own proprietary battery and its matching charger. Lithium-ions typically have great capacity and hold their charge for a long time, but you might want to buy an extra battery—you can't use readily available alkalines as a backup. See Figure 1-5.

Figure 1-5. High-performance batteries such as Lithium-ions (pictured on the left and right) and NiMH (center) will power your digital camera many times longer than alkalines ever could. The only problem is that many compact digicams have small batteries (left) that sometimes fade before you've finished a day's shooting. Figure the cost of an extra battery into the overall price of your camera. And don't forget to take the charger on trips lasting longer than a day.

Exposure Meter ⓑⓘⓐ

The exposure meter reads the light passing through the lens and determines the proper shutter speed and aperture to produce a well-exposed picture.

All digital cameras have some type of exposure meter, but many models have more than one *pattern* for measuring light. The three most common patterns are *center-weighted*, *evaluative*, and *spot*, and are shown in more detail in Figure 1-6. Advanced cameras may include all three of these metering patterns, while more basic models may rely on center-weighted or evaluative.

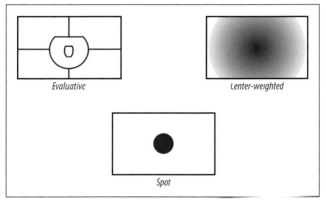

Figure 1-6. Three common metering patterns. The pattern on the top left is commonly called "evaluative" because light is measured in each area, then evaluated by the camera's built-in computer. The diagram on the right shows a center-weighted pattern. The bottom figure is a typical "spot metering" pattern, where the camera reads only the light in the center area of the frame and ignores everything else.

Evaluative ❸ ❶. The image area is divided into sections (usually six or more), and light is measured in each section. The camera then "evaluates" each section and matches the overall pattern to data stored in its computer system. The resulting camera settings are determined by how the pattern and data match up.

Center-weighted ❸. The entire picture area is measured by the meter, with extra emphasis placed on subjects in the center of the frame.

Spot ❶. Only the center area of the viewing area, usually indicated by brackets, measures light to determine the exposure. Spot metering is helpful in contrast lighting situations that might fool other metering patterns.

Image Sensor ❸❶Ⓐ

The image sensor converts light energy passing through the camera lens into a digital signal. The most common sensors are CCDs (Charged-Coupled Devices). But many cameras, such as the Canon SLRs, are now employing Complementary Metal Oxide Semiconductor (CMOS) sensors that have many of the attributes of CCD types, but use less energy. And recently, a third type of sensor called the Foveon X3 has entered the market and is the current choice for Sigma SLRs. The Foveon sensor is a type of CMOS, but with a much different design. It actually uses three separate layers of pixel sensors embedded in silicon. CCD and traditional CMOS sensors have a single layer.

How concerned should you be about the type of sensor in the camera that you're considering (or have just purchased)? Type isn't as important as size, or, more specifically, how many *pixels* (picture elements) it supports. All three types

---

PRO TIP

New Digital SLR Format: The Four-Thirds System

This is a proposed standard for digital SLR cameras that employ a four-thirds image sensor. Major proponents of this system are Olympus, Kodak, and Fuji. Four-thirds refers to the proportions of the image sensor producing images that are 4:3 in dimension, such as 1600x1200 pixels. The goal of this system is to establish a common standard for lens mounts. The Olympus E-1 is the first four-thirds digital SLR.

---

of sensors support millions of pixels, and the term *megapixel* means just that: a million pixels. So instead of saying, "I just bought a camera with a sensor that supports 2,000,000 pixels," you can say, "I just bought a two-megapixel camera."

Consumer cameras range in capacity from 1.3 to 6 megapixels. Pro cameras have sensors as large as 14 megapixels. Generally speaking, you want at least 2 megapixels for snap shooting and vacation pictures. The more megapixels your camera has, the bigger the prints you can make. Two-megapixel cameras can produce photo-quality prints up to 5×7"; 3-megapixel models are good up to 8×10"; and 4-megapixel advanced digicams can produce very nice 11×14" prints.

If your main goal is to produce pictures to send via email or for posting on your web site, cameras in the 1.3-megapixel range ❾ should be fine. But if you like to make prints of your digital images, see Table 1-1 for your ideal camera.

Table 1-1. Quality ranges of common digicams

Camera type	2MP ❶	3MP ❶	4MP ❹	5MP ❹
Photo quality	5×7	8×10	11×14	12×16
Acceptable	8×10	11×14	12×16	16×20

Memory Cards ❽

Memory cards store the picture data captured by your camera. Nearly every digital camera contains some type of removable memory. When the camera takes a picture and creates the data for that image, it "writes" that information on the memory card. This enables you to retrieve or transfer your electronic pictures long after they've been recorded.

The most popular type of card is CompactFlash (CF), but Sony Memory Stick (MS), IBM MicroDrive, MultimediaCard (MMC), Secure Digital (SD), and the latest entry, xD-Picture Card introduced by Fuji and Olympus, are all capable alternatives. Some older cameras use SmartMedia (SM) cards, which are still readily available. But that technology is being replaced by the xD-Picture Card, which is smaller and has more capacity.

Figure 1-7 shows an Olympus C-5050 camera that accepts four types of media. You can use any of the types at any given time, switch between cards for recording pictures, and even copy images between cards (which provides an "in-camera" backup of your shots).

Figure 1-7. The Olympus C-5050 accepts four types of media: CompactFlash (left), xD-Picture Card (center), SmartMedia (right), and the IBM Microdrive (in the camera).

The type of memory card your digicam accepts isn't as important as its capacity. Most cameras ship with *starter memory cards* that hold only 16 or 32MB. These are fine during the learning phase, but once you're ready to take your camera on vacation or photograph your daughter's birthday party, you'll need more memory.

Table 1-2 can help you determine the best capacity for your camera, based on its megapixels.

Table 1-2. Minimum and recommended digicam memory cards

Camera type (megapixels)	2MP	3MP	4MP and up
Minimum card (megabytes)	64MB	128MB	256MB
Recommended card	128MB	256MB	512MB

One other thing to consider when shopping for memory cards is the speed at which they read and write. "High-Speed" or "Ultra" cards can perform at twice the speed or more compared to "Standard" cards. Much of this benefit depends on the sophistication of your camera's electronics. Basic consumer point-and-shoot models typically don't benefit from high-speed cards as much as advanced amateur and pro cameras. If you have a high-performance camera, you should consider having at least one high-speed memory card. Standard cards should perform just fine for point-and-shoots and other basic models.

Mass storage USB ❶. Enables the camera to be connected to a computer without using any special drivers, much in the same way an external hard drive is mounted by plugging it in. You can then "drag and drop" your pictures from the camera to the computer, or use an image application to download them.

Digital cameras that are USB Mass Storage devices can be connected to computers running the following operating systems without installing any software: Windows XP, 2000, ME, and 98 SE, plus Macintosh 9.x and Mac OS X 10.1 or later.

RAM buffer ❶. Stores image data in the camera's Random Access Memory (RAM) before transferring it to the memory card. The RAM buffer enables advanced functionality, such as burst and movie modes. The camera can move picture data to the RAM buffer much faster than writing it to the memory card. So when you use burst mode, for example, the camera captures a sequence of shots in the

RAM buffer, then transfers the data to the memory card after you've released the shutter button. RAM buffers can be as large as 32MB. The larger the buffer, the longer your shot sequences can be.

Self-timer ❽. Delays the shutter release for approximately 10 seconds. Activating the self-timer is an easy way for the photographer to join a group shot. Sometimes this function is used instead of a remote release to trip the shutter without jarring the camera. This is especially useful in low-light situations with slow shutter speeds when the camera is mounted on a tripod.

Video-out connection ❶. Allows you to connect the camera directly to a television or other monitor to display pictures on a larger screen. Using video out is an easy way to show your pictures to a large group of people.

Putting It All Together

Now that you're familiar with the features of your digital camera, how do you use them to take great pictures? In the next chapter, What Does It Do?, you'll learn helpful techniques such as how to master the focus lock, choose the right flash setting, and use "burst mode" to capture action shots—plus lots more. Great pictures are only a chapter away.

What Does It Do?

Now that you're familiar with your camera's basic components, you can concentrate on how to unlock their picture-taking magic. For example, a simple flash menu button (⚡) allows you to cycle through a series of versatile lighting controls. But what do they mean, and which one should you choose?

In this chapter, you'll learn how to use those seemingly simple buttons and dials to tap the incredible picture-taking capacity hidden within your digital camera.

Taking Control of Buttons, Dials, and Menus

This section covers camera controls alphabetically from A to Z, or more specifically, from Aperture to Zooming. New terms are listed in *italic*. If you're not sure where to find any of these settings on your particular camera, double-check the owner's manual or refer to Chapter 1 of this guide.

As always, it's best to have your camera in hand as you work with the text and study the photo examples. The more you shoot, the more natural these techniques will become.

Aperture Priority Mode (AV)

Many intermediate and advanced cameras allow you to choose the aperture setting, and the camera sets the proper corresponding shutter speed. This setting is sometimes denoted as *AV*, which stands for *aperture value*. You can typically access this setting via the Mode Dial or as a menu option.

Choose the aperture priority mode when you want to control *depth of field*. In other words, how much of your picture, from front to back, do you want in focus? Shallow depth of field is often used for portraits—your subject is in focus, but everything else is a little soft. Choose an aperture value of 2.0, 2.8, or 4 for this type of shooting situation. The lower the value, the shallower the depth of field; meaning that less of the image will be in focus (see Table 2-1 for specific depth-of-field settings).

Table 2-1. Depth-of-field settings

f-stop	Diameter of aperture	Depth of field	Background looks
f-2	Very large diameter	Very shallow	Very soft
f-2.8	Large diameter	Shallow	Soft
f-4	Medium diameter	Moderate	A little out of focus
f-5.6	Medium diameter	Moderate	A little out of focus
f-8	Small diameter	Moderately deep	Mostly in focus
f-11	Small diameter	Deep	Sharp
f-16	Very small diameter	Very deep	Very sharp

When shooting landscapes, you'll probably want "deep" depth of field, which produces a sharp image from foreground to background. Choose an aperture value of 8, 11, or 16 for deeper depth of field.

Autoexposure

See *Programmed Autoexposure*.

Burst/Continuous Shooting Mode

All but the most basic cameras have some sort of *burst* or *continuous shooting* mode (▢, indicated by layers of rectangles). Typically

Shooting an Outdoor Portrait with a Soft Background

If your camera has a portrait-shooting mode, it's designed to "open up" the aperture to provide a shallow depth of field. See Figure 2-1 for an example. Or, you can use aperture priority and select f-2, f-2.5, or f-2.8. Place the subject at least 10 feet away from the background, more if possible. This will soften the background detail, putting more emphasis on your subject. Set your zoom lens to the telephoto position (this enhances the soft background effect even more). Focus on the model's eyes. Press the shutter halfway to "lock" the focus. While still holding the shutter in the halfway position, recompose so the composition is just the way you want it. Then take the picture. If the lighting on the model's face isn't to your liking, force the flash on (see the entry for *Flash Modes* later in this chapter), and shoot again. This setup should provide a nicely focused model against a softened background.

Figure 2-1. Soft background portrait captured with Canon 10D and 85mm, f-1.8 lens set to f-2.

this mode is a menu option, but some cameras display it as a button option that you can access at any time. Either way, it allows you to shoot a series of pictures while holding the shutter button in the down position—see Figure 2-2. The number of pictures you can record in one burst is determined by the capacity of your camera's *RAM buffer*.

Most people use this continuous shooting feature for recording sports events. And it is a great choice for capturing a baseball player's swing or a quarterback's touchdown pass. But burst modes can also help you compensate for *shutter lag*—that diabolical delay from the moment you press the shutter to when the picture is actually recorded. Some digital cameras have shutter lags as long as two seconds, which is a lifetime in action photography.

The key to overcoming shutter lag by using burst mode is to start the sequence just before the action begins, then shoot continuously until the buffer fills up. By doing so, you greatly increase your chances of capturing the decisive moment.

Figure 2-2. Burst mode—this short series was taken with continuous mode on. The sequence was started as the horse and carriage approached. Then, upon review, it's just a matter of choosing the best image in the series, and either archiving or discarding the rest of the shots.

PRACTICAL EXAMPLE

Capturing the Decisive Moment

To catch the perfect moment, you should set your camera to *continuous* or *burst* mode. Take, for example, an event such as your son blowing out the candles on his fifth birthday. First, make sure the activity is in a well-lit room, or even better, outdoors (and turn your flash off—flashes can't fire fast enough to keep pace with burst modes). Focus on the child and hold the shutter down halfway to "lock it in." Still holding the shutter in the halfway position, recompose. Start the series as he prepares to blow out the candles and shoot continuously until the RAM buffer fills up and the camera stops taking pictures. You'll have to wait a moment for the camera to process all the information you've just recorded. Then go back through the sequence and choose the picture that best depicts the decisive moment. You can either erase the others to save memory card space, or keep them to show the entire sequence.

Close-Ups

Digital cameras are great for getting in real tight with your subject. This is sometimes referred to as *macro photography*. Unlike most film cameras, digicams usually have the macro capability built right into the camera—you don't need any special accessories for impressive close-ups. Usually you can access the macro mode by pressing the button that has the "flower" icon next to it (❁). Some cameras may bury this option in the onscreen menu and force you to dig a little bit to find it. But keep looking; it's in there somewhere.

The main thing to remember with close-up photography is that whenever you increase lens magnification, you have to hold the camera extra steady to prevent camera shake, which can make your picture look out of focus due to too much camera movement during the exposure. For important close-ups that you plan on printing, you may even want to steady the camera using a tripod. The rule of thumb is this:

Increased magnification means increased camera shake.

Taking a Close-Up of a Flower

Put your camera on a tripod. Turn on the close-up mode and turn off your flash (many digital camera flashes overexpose subjects at very close range). Focus your camera on the most important element in the composition and hold the shutter halfway down to lock in the focus. While still holding the shutter in the halfway position, recompose if you need to, then shoot the picture (see Figure 2-3). If there's a breeze blowing, wait for a calm moment before shooting: your picture will be sharper. Review your work after a few shots, then make any necessary adjustments. If you have a manual focus option on your camera, you can compose your picture first, then manually focus. Use the self-timer or the remote release to trip the shutter—that will prevent you from jarring the camera when you take the shot.

Figure 2-3. Close-up shot of a Japanese Anemone flower. The focus is set on the orange pistils. Notice that because of the shallow depth of field, the background leaves fall out of focus quickly. This is due to the increased magnification of close-up photography.

Your depth of field is very shallow in close-up photography, so be sure to focus on the element that is most important to you. If you have an aperture priority mode, you can increase the depth of field a little more by setting the aperture to f-11, f-16, or f-22. The higher the f-stop setting, the more depth of field you'll have.

Composition

Whether you're using the LCD monitor or the optical viewfinder, the composition of your picture determines a large part of its success. *Composition* is the arrangement of the elements in your photograph. The subject, the horizon line, and the background elements all play a role in successful composition. And this is just as true with a basic point-and-shoot camera as it is with a top-of-the-line Nikon digital SLR.

The first step to creating great photographs is to consider all elements in your viewfinder. Here are a few questions to consider when framing your picture: Where is the subject placed? Are there any distracting background elements such as telephone poles? Is the horizon line straight? Should you raise the camera angle or lower it?

Most photographers keep five rules of thumb in mind when composing their shots. These are not hard-and-fast rules, but they are worth remembering and applying as often as possible.

Get closer. Use your feet and your zoom lens to frame your subject as tightly as possible. Once you get closer and compose your image, take a few shots, then get closer again. Your pictures will improve dramatically.

Remember the Rule of Thirds. Don't always put your subject dead center in the frame. Instead, divide the frame into thirds, both horizontally and vertically (like a tic-tac-toe board), and position the important elements along those lines. Your compositions will be less static and more interesting.

Eliminate busy backgrounds. Trees are great, but not when they're growing out of the tops of people's heads. Look out for busy patterns, bright objects, and other distracting elements.

Analyzing a Landscape Composition

When you first look at Figure 2-4, you'll most likely find the image pleasing. But why? There are a number of compositional rules in effect here that contribute to the success of the photograph. Notice the first element in the image your eye goes to—the gun tower. By placing it in the left third of the composition with a diagonal line leading to it (the fence), you can actually direct the viewer's eye to where you want it to go first. The solid background of trees doesn't distract from the fort, yet provides some nice color and texture for the shot. Two large eucalyptus trees on either side of the fort serve as a frame to help direct the eye inward. Also notice that the foreground, which is composed to also help pull the viewer's eye inward, is slightly soft. If you prefer a sharper foreground, simply increase your depth of field by choosing an aperture of f-16 or so, and focus on the bend in the fence.

Figure 2-4: This image seems simple when you first look at it, but there are many compositional rules in effect that contribute to its success.

Go high, go low. Change your camera angle when working a shot. Get low on the ground and shoot upward. Raise the camera over your head and shoot down—swiveling lenses and LCD monitors make this easier than ever.

Simple is better. Try not to clutter your compositions with non-essential elements. Keep things simple, move in close, and find an interesting arrangement.

Compression or Image Quality

Another way in which digital cameras are much different from their film counterparts is that they actually let you set the *quality of the image* via the *compression* or *image quality* setting. All digital cameras save images as some form of Joint Photographic Experts Group (JPEG) file. If you've worked with JPEG files, you know that you can save them at various quality levels, usually from 1 to 12. A JPEG saved at level 1 has both very poor quality and a very small file size—it is said to be *highly compressed*. The same file saved at level 12 has excellent image quality, but the corresponding file size is quite large—it is *minimally compressed*.

Your digital camera gives you some of these same options in the compression or image quality setting, which is usually one of the first items you'll see when you open the onscreen menu. Instead of providing you with number values such as "3," "6," and "9," cameras use terms such as *basic*, *normal*, and *fine*, or *normal*, *fine*, and *super-fine*. Regardless of the actual terms used, pay attention to the order in which they are listed.

- *Basic* or *normal* is low resolution and should be avoided, because it limits your ability to make good prints. Don't be tempted by the number of extra pictures you can squeeze on a card using low resolution—it is much better to buy a bigger memory card instead.

- *Normal* or *fine* is medium resolution and is acceptable for emailing pictures or images for the Web. You can also make decent prints from images at this setting.

- *Fine* or *superfine* is the highest resolution setting on your camera and the one you should consider using all the time. True, you can't squeeze as many pictures on to your memory card as you would using the lower resolution settings, but you're capturing images at their highest quality and will always have the option to produce quality prints or large web images from all of your shots.

Some cameras also provide a *RAW* or *TIFF* resolution setting. These settings don't use any compression and produce very large file sizes. If you know that the final product is going to be a large print or a picture in a magazine, then these settings are worth considering. But for everyday shooting, they might be overkill. See Working with RAW files on page 97 for more information.

For general shooting, you should be happy with the quality of your pictures set at the highest compressed level, which is usually *fine* or *superfine*. See Figure 2-5.

Figure 2-5. Compression levels: in this menu the "S" stands for "superfine," which is this camera's highest quality setting.

Continuous Shooting Mode

See *Burst/Continuous Shooting Mode*.

Deleting Images

See *Erasing Images*.

Digital Zoom

Unlike the *optical zoom* on your camera, which consists of actual glass elements, the *digital zoom* is a function of the camera's electronics. By enabling the digital zoom, you can increase the magnification of your lens to bring your subjects even closer than is possible with just the optics alone.

The tradeoff is that you compromise image quality when you use the digital zoom. Since it's a function of the camera's electronics and not the actual lens, the digital zoom is really emulating the telephoto effect instead of actually recording the image at that optical magnification. So even though you "get closer" by using the digital zoom, there's some quality loss too.

For normal, everyday shooting you should avoid using the digital zoom. But when you encounter situations where getting the shot is more important than a little quality loss, the digital zoom can be a very helpful tool.

Reminder: Don't base a camera-buying decision on the digital zoom rating. Consider only the optical zoom numbers.

Erasing Images

There are two types of erasing. Most photographers use the *single erase* option when they take a bad picture and want to get rid of it to free up space on the memory card. Cameras usually have a "trash" button for this procedure. The other type of erasing is the *Erase All* command, which wipes every picture off your card, usually after you've just uploaded them to your computer. The Erase All command is usually a menu item. You can also use the *Format Card* command, but before using either method to wipe the memory card clean, double-check that you have indeed uploaded your pictures to your computer.

As for single erase: sometimes photographers discard images too quickly before fully examining them. Obviously some pictures need to go right away—if you're in a dark room and the flash doesn't fire, it's a pretty safe bet to dump that shot. But if you take a series of images and want to erase all but the best, then make sure you carefully examine the others. Many digital cameras provide a magnify function for the LCD monitor. Try zooming in on your potential discards and examine them closely before pressing the trash button. To be extra safe, view them on the computer, then trash them if they still don't make the cut. You can miss subtle details when viewing pictures on the tiny LCD monitor, and sometimes those very details make a great shot.

Reminder: Never use your computer to format a memory card. Instead, use the Format Card command on your camera. This will ensure the best communication between the memory card and your camera.

Exposure Compensation

One of the most valuable tools available on your digital camera is the *exposure compensation* scale, which allows you to override your camera's autoexposure reading so you can capture the image exactly the way you want it. On some cameras, this is a button option that you can get to easily, and on others it's a menu item that's not quite as convenient. Either way, you'll want to know where exposure compensation is on your camera—it can help you take pictures that more accurately represent the scene you're capturing and save you time later on the computer when adjusting the exposure.

You may be thinking, "But doesn't my camera always know the right exposure to set?" Not entirely. The light meter in your camera is calibrated to expose properly for anything that's 18 percent gray. This represents the approximate light reflection of a deep blue sky or green foliage, which is the most common background in outdoor shots. And indeed, your light meter works great most of the time.

But what if you want to shoot a pretty table setting that has a white tablecloth? It's not 18 percent gray; it's white! If you don't override your camera's light meter via exposure compensation, then guess what shade your camera will render that tablecloth—18 percent gray. In effect, your automatic wonder digicam has *underexposed* the table setting. Figures 2-6 and 2-7 show an underexposed and properly exposed shot of a table.

You can use your camera's exposure compensation option to render the image correctly. When you find the control, you'll see a scale with "0" in the middle, "plus" numbers to the right, and "negative" numbers to the left.

Figure 2-6. Underexposed composition influenced by the white tablecloth.

Figure 2-7. Properly exposed table setting: exposure compensation control set to +1.

When you're shooting an object that's very bright, such as a white tablecloth, you want to *add* more exposure to render it white. So, move the pointer on the exposure scale to +1 (see Figure 2-8).

```
-2  .  .  1  .  .  0  .  .  +1  .  .  +2
```

Figure 2-8. Exposure compensation scale.

On the other hand, if you're shooting a very dark object with your camera in autoexposure mode, the camera tends to overexpose the shot and render the object lighter than it really is. In this situation, you should subtract exposure by moving the pointer on the exposure scale to −1. See Figures 2-9 and 2-10 for examples.

As you become more comfortable with using the exposure compensation function, you can make more subtle adjustments to your pictures. You can also fine-tune your images later in Photoshop or another editor, but the more accurately you capture your pictures in the first place, the less time you'll have to spend processing them later.

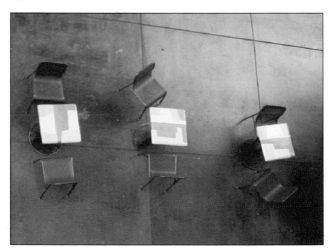

Figure 2-9. Overexposed dark object.

Figure 2-10. Properly exposed dark object: exposure compensation pointer set to –1.

Exposure Lock

Typically, when you press the shutter button halfway and hold it there, the camera locks in both the *focus* and the *exposure*. While still holding the button halfway down, you can then recompose the shot and take the picture. But you might want to lock the focus on one element and the exposure on another.

Some cameras allow you to lock the exposure independently of the focus. If your camera has this function, it usually works like this: first, you press the shutter button halfway to take a meter reading; then, while still holding the shutter button down, you press another button to lock in the exposure. An indicator usually appears on the LCD screen to let you know you've locked the exposure. Now you can focus on another element and take the picture. Remember to turn off the exposure lock once you're done working with that particular shot.

You can use exposure lock as a shortcut for exposure compensation. Instead of accessing the exposure scale and adjusting your image that way, you can find a middle tone in the picture you want to shoot, such as a patch of grass, and lock your exposure on it. This is a faster way to override your camera's autoexposure setting in difficult lighting situations.

Exposure Metering

Most digital cameras rely on *programmed autoexposure* metering to set the aperture and shutter speed. Essentially, the camera's light meter "reads" the light and compares the data to a set of instructions stored in the camera's memory. The camera then chooses the best aperture/shutter-speed combination based on the data it receives from the light meter.

The most important thing you need to know about exposure metering is that cameras are not perfect when it comes to evaluating exposure. They are most often fooled when presented with very bright or very dark subjects.

Fortunately, most cameras allow you to override the programmed exposure setting. See the entry for *Exposure Compensation*.

File Format

JPEG is the format used by most digital cameras. JPEG files are very portable and can be read by nearly every computer and web browser. JPEG files use compression to keep the file size small for easy transport. Users can determine the amount of compression by selecting options from the menu function on their digital cameras—usually "high," "medium," and "low," but not always using those exact terms. For example, the terms "superfine," "fine," and "normal" are sometimes used instead. See the *Compression or Image Quality* entry for more detail about these settings.

Over the last few years, a specialized version of JPEG has emerged for digital camera use. Exchangeable Image File (EXIF) has the same compression properties as standard JPEGs, but allows the camera to record additional data to the picture file—such as shutter speed, aperture, and date—that can be "read" by most modern image editors. This additional information is sometimes referred to as *metadata*, and it's a real blessing for photographers who want access to the technical specifications for every shot they record, but hate taking notes. The current EXIF version is 2.1.

Tagged Image File Format (TIFF) settings are sometimes available as an alternate "high quality" format. As used on digital cameras, TIFFs are not usually compressed, so file sizes are very large. For general shooting, using the "high quality" JPEG setting is just fine. But for those special situations when you want to squeeze every drop of quality from the image, the TIFF setting might be appropriate.

Some camera makers also provide a "RAW" format option that is also uncompressed. As with TIFFs, the file sizes are large, and the quality is very high. RAW is good choice for the most accurate color fidelity because you can delay your white balance choice until later, while working on the computer. But keep in mind that it might take longer for your camera to write information to the memory card when using this format, and you might need a special application to work with these images on your computer. See Working with RAW Files on page 97 for more information.

Film Speed

See *ISO Speed*.

Flash Compensation

This feature enables you to manually adjust the flash exposure, and is more common on advanced cameras than basic point-and-shoots. Much in the same way that exposure compensation gives you a tool for fine-tuning your camera's programmed autoexposure, flash compensation provides a way to increase or decrease light output from your flash. So if your subject is too bright (overexposed) after you take a test shot, you can set flash compensation to -1 to decrease output. On the other hand, if your model is rendered too dark after taking the first shot, you can set flash compensation to +1 to increase light output.

Flash Modes

The default flash mode for most cameras is automatic, and that's where it stays for most folks. But even the most basic digicams offer multiple flash settings that can help you take engaging photos under a variety of lighting conditions. Some of the typical flash settings that you might encounter on your camera are:

Auto. The camera activates the flash as determined by the light meter reading. If you're indoors in low light, the flash fires. Outside on a bright sunny day? The camera turns the flash off.

Red-eye reduction. Many digicams have some sort of red-eye reduction mode. Red eye occurs when the subject's eyes are dilated (in dim lighting), exposing the retina. When the light from the flash reflects off the retina, the resulting color is red. Most cameras tackle this problem by shining a light at the subject before the flash goes off. The thinking here is that the pre-flash will cause the pupils to constrict, which may reduce the chance of red eye.

The challenge for a photographer using red-eye reduction flash modes is coping with the extended delay from the time the shutter button is pressed until the actual picture is recorded. If you use red-eye reduction, remind the subject to hold the pose until the final flash has fired. And remember to hold the camera steady during this entire process.

Auto red-eye reduction. The combination of auto and red-eye reduction modes. The camera uses red-eye reduction whenever it determines that flash is required.

Flash on. This setting is usually referred to as *fill flash*. The camera will fire the flash with every exposure regardless of the light meter reading. *Flash on* is one of the most useful camera settings you have because it allows you to take professional-looking portraits outdoors by adding enough light to properly illuminate the subject while balancing the exposure for the background. The result is a beautiful image with all components properly exposed. See Figure 2-11.

Flash off. Sometimes the flash destroys the mood of a shot. This is particularly true with indoor portraits where the subject is next to a window with daylight streaming in. Creative photographers like to turn off the flash in these settings, steady the camera, and record an *existing light* photograph that captures the mood of the setting.

Slow-synchro flash. Often referred to as *nighttime* mode, this setting tells your camera to use a slow shutter speed in combination with the flash. By doing this, you can capture more background detail in dimly lit scenes, such as portraits shot at twilight, or in an indoor shooting where you want to capture the mood of the setting in addition to having your main subject properly exposed by the flash. Remember to hold the camera very steady when using slow-synchro flash to prevent blurring of the background. If you have a tripod, you may want to use it for these types of shots.

Figure 2-11. Flash on (or fill flash) can improve your outdoor portraits.

Taking Control of Buttons, Dials, and Menus

To Flash or Not to Flash

The two most valuable flash modes are flash on and flash off. Yes, auto flash is fine for most situations, but sometimes you have to override auto mode to capture the shot you want. Outdoor portraits, for example, look great when you enable the flash on mode. The camera will automatically balance the background exposure and supply just the right amount of flash to perfectly illuminate your subject (see Figure 2-11). Just remember to work within flash range, which is 8–10 feet for most cameras.

In other situations, such as for indoor portraits, you may want to turn the flash off and use existing lighting (see Figure 2-12). Doing so will give your picture pleasing soft tones without any hot spots from the flash. You'll need to steady the camera, however, to compensate for a much slower shutter speed. If you don't have a tripod, place your camera on a table or another flat surface. You may even want to use the self-timer so you don't jar the camera during exposure. Remind the model to hold still during exposure so as not to blur the picture.

Focus Lock

One of the most common pitfalls with point-and-shoot cameras is their tendency to focus on the object that is not your intended subject. Instead of capturing your best friend perfectly exposed in and focus, the back wall 10 feet away is sharp as a tack, while your buddy is a fuzzy blob in the foreground. The odds for this scenario increase if your buddy is standing off to one side of the frame.

You can prevent the blurring of your buddy by using focus lock. Simply point your camera directly at the primary subject, then press the shutter button down halfway until the focus confirmation light goes on. Continue holding the shutter button down in the halfway position and recompose your shot. Then take the picture.

Figure 2-12. In certain indoor situations, you may want to turn the flash off to capture pleasing soft tones.

Format Memory Card

Often included as a menu item, *Format Memory Card* is an alternative to *Erase All Pictures*. Either procedure clears your memory card of all images so you can shoot more pictures, but Format Memory Card also customizes the memory card for your camera by writing a small amount of data to it. This is a good option to choose before you start using a new memory card, or if you're switching memory cards from another camera. You'll enjoy better performance if you format your memory card in the camera, rather than in the computer.

Infinity Lock

Some cameras have an *infinity setting* that allows you to "lock" the focus on subjects that are 10 feet away or farther. At first this might not seem like an overly useful addition to your camera's feature set, but infinity lock is particularly handy in situations when your camera's auto focus system has difficulty "locking in" on a subject, causing it to "hunt" as it searches for the correct setting. In this case, you simply select the infinity lock and shoot away.

Infinity lock helps reduce *shutter lag* too. If, for example, you're taking pictures at your daughter's soccer game and are missing too many shots because of the lag between the time you press the shutter button and moment the picture is actually recorded, then try the infinity lock. The camera is now pre-focused and will respond more quickly.

If you're shooting landscapes through a car or train window and the camera is having a hard time focusing through the glass, then enabling the infinity lock feature should solve your problem.

ISO Speed

Sometimes referred to as "film speed," *ISO speed* is actually a better term for expressing the light sensitivity of your digital camera. ISO stands for International Organization for Standardization. This entity has established many standards, including the light sensitivity of photographic materials.

If your camera has multiple ISO speed settings, you can use these adjustments to increase the light sensitivity of the image sensor. The default setting for most digicams is ISO 100. (See Figure 2-13.) This is the speed setting for general photography. If you're in a low-light situation and need to increase the sensitivity of your image sensor, change the ISO speed setting from 100 to 200, or even 400 if necessary. Each setting is the equivalent to one f-stop of light.

Figure 2-13. Keep your ISO setting on 100 or "Auto" for general shooting.

Keep in mind, though, that increasing the ISO speed also increases *image noise*, which decreases the quality of your picture. Sometimes this tradeoff is worth it, but for everyday shooting, make sure your ISO speed setting is 100 or lower.

Reminder: If you do increase the ISO speed for a special situation, be sure to change the setting back to 100 right after the shoot. You will be sorely disappointed if you photograph a beautiful landscape the next day at ISO 400.

JPEG

See *File Format*.

Macro Mode

See *Close-Ups*.

Magnify Control

See *Zoom/Magnify Control*.

Manual Exposure Setting

Many digital cameras allow only programmed autoexposure, but more advanced models also provide complete control over the aperture and speed settings. If your camera has this option, it's probably denoted as *Manual*, or *Manual Exposure*.

In traditional film photography, switching to *manual mode* was a true rite of passage. The photographer would fiddle with the aperture and shutter speed settings, then hope that the pictures were properly exposed when returned from the photo finisher. This process was by no means for the faint of heart. But digital photography has changed all of that, and manual mode is now much more friendly because you can preview the final result on the LCD monitor before you press the shutter button. Now manual mode represents both control and convenience.

For outdoor photography, start by setting your shutter speed to 1/125th of a second and the aperture to f-8. Preview the scene in your LCD monitor. If the image looks too dark, then "open up" the aperture to f-5.6 or "slow down" the shutter speed to 1/60th of a second. You'll see the results of your adjustments in real time on the LCD monitor. If the scene is too bright, then "stop down" the aperture to f-11 or "speed up" the shutter to 1/250th of a second.

This is the beauty of manual mode photography; you have the option to adjust either the aperture or the shutter speed to reach the desired result. Sometimes aperture is more important, such as for portraits where you want to soften the background. In that case, set the aperture on f-2.0 or f-2.8 (wide open) and change the shutter speed until the image looks correct in the LCD monitor.

Other times shutter speed might be more important, such as when "stopping the action" during a sporting event: set the shutter speed at 1/500th of a second and adjust the aperture until the image looks properly exposed.

With a little practice, you'll find that manual exposure is an easy way for you to be in complete control of your digital camera.

Movie Mode

Digital still cameras are versatile imaging tools; many provide the option to capture short video clips, sometimes with sound. Typically you access this function via the *Movie Mode* setting.

"Short" is the operative word here. Many cameras allow you to capture only 30 seconds of video at a time. After it captures the sequence, the camera writes the data to the memory card and allows you to capture another 30 seconds until the memory card is full.

After you upload these video clips to your computer, you can stitch them together using a video editor such as QuickTime Pro. Standard size for these short movies is 320 pixels wide by 240 pixels tall. Typical frame rate is 15 frames per second (fps), which is half the speed of standard video, but still quite decent.

More advanced cameras enable you to capture longer sequences, sometimes three minutes or longer and usually with sound, via the microphone port located on the front of the camera. You can preview these mini-movies on your LCD monitor, and if you like them, you can post them to your personal web site or send them as email attachments.

For best image quality when shooting video, remember these tips:

Hold the camera steady during filming. Tripods are best for video shooting, but in a pinch, you can use your neck strap to stabilize the camera. Hold the camera out from your body until the strap is taut. Keep the camera in this position during filming, and it will help steady your shots.

Shoot in good lighting. Even more than with still photography, video requires good lighting. If your scene doesn't have enough ambient light, consider adding some with an additional light source.

Frame your subjects tight. Keep in mind that the final size of your movies is only 320 pixels wide and 240 pixels tall to begin with, so you can't afford to stand too far back from the action or your subjects will be ant-sized. Get close and shoot tight.

Your digital still camera won't replace a good video camcorder, but in a pinch it can capture a special moment that you would have otherwise missed.

Panorama Mode

If you want to capture the breadth of a scene, you most likely won't be able to fit all the grandeur into your camera's viewfinder—even at the wide-angle setting. Have you ever remarked to someone viewing your vacation pictures, "It sure looked a lot more impressive when I was standing there"?

Panorama mode is a clever alternative offered by camera makers to help you capture the grandeur of big landscapes. The magic happens by photographing a sequence of images, then "stitching" them together later with your computer. Panorama mode prepares the sequence of shots for easy assemblage. Cameras that have this option also include the corresponding software required to make seamless final images. If your camera didn't come with stitching software, you can use Photoshop Elements, a terrific all-purpose image editor that costs less than $100.

Most panoramas require three to six images to achieve the full effect. When looking for good subjects, keep in mind that it's easier to create a seamless image when your subject is evenly illuminated. That usually means that the sun is to your back or off one shoulder. Avoid shooting directly into the sun for any of the frames in the sequence, at least until you're a little more experienced.

Then next trick is to keep the horizon line as level as possible when you capture each frame in the sequence. Tripods help tremendously with this task, but you might not always have one with you. So the next best solution is to become a *human tripod*. Here's how the technique works:

- Hold the camera firmly with both hands so you can see through the optical viewfinder or LCD monitor.

- Press your elbows against your body to create a steady support for the camera.

- Compose your first picture, usually starting from the left side. Note the location of the horizon line and make sure it's level.

- Take the first shot. After the shutter has fired, don't move!

- Continue to hold the camera in the locked elbow position and rotate your body a few degrees to the right to compose the next frame in the sequence. The only moving body parts should be your feet—everything else should be still as night. Make sure you have a 30 percent overlap from the previous image you shot—the computer uses this overlap information to stitch the pictures together.

- Check the horizon line to make sure it's in the same location as the last frame, and that it's still level.

- Take the second shot. (Don't move afterward!)

- Repeat this procedure through the entire sequence of shots.

- Turn off panorama mode once you've finished the series.

With a little practice, the human tripod technique will yield fantastic panoramas without lugging around your favorite three-legged friend. See Figure 2-14.

One last thing to keep in mind is that panoramas are stunning as large prints. Shoot these sequences at your camera's highest resolution so you always have the option to print them at maximum size.

Partial Metering Area

See *Spot Meter*.

Photo Effects

Many cameras allow you to apply creative effects—such as black and white, sepia toned, vivid color, and low sharpening—instead of the standard color image. You can apply those effects in the camera using the effects settings, or convert your standard color images using the computer after you've uploaded the images—it's your choice. Here are the most common effects modes and what they do. See Figure 2-15 for some example photos.

Black and white. Captures the picture as a grayscale image, eliminating all color.

Blackboard. Underexposes the image, making sure that the blackboard (with chalk writing) is black and not gray.

Figure 2-14. This image of the Bay Bridge from San Francisco is actually six images "stitched" together.

— **What Does It Do?**

Low sharpening. Softens the outlines of the subject. This is a good effect to experiment with for portraits. The effect isn't as strong as with a softening filter that goes over the lens, but this setting is effective.

Sepia toned. Adds a warmish brown tone to the image. Unlike black and white, which is easy to apply in the computer, sepia toning is easier to use as an in-camera effect. You might want to take a second shot in full color as a backup.

Figure 2-15. The first photo was captured in standard color mode. The second image applies the sepia effect, and the third uses the black and white effect.

Vivid color. Enhances the color saturation of the picture. This can also be easily accomplished with the computer later, but this effect is handy because you can use your camera's LCD monitor to preview how a highly saturated image will look.

Whiteboard. Overexposes the image so you can use the digital camera to capture notes off a whiteboard or photograph posters with white backgrounds.

Programmed Autoexposure

The most common method for setting the aperture and shutter speed for digital cameras is *programmed autoexposure*. On many basic and intermediate models, this is the only exposure mode offered.

When using programmed exposure, all you have to do is "point and shoot." The camera's light meter "reads" the scene and compares that information to data stored in the camera's electronics. The camera then selects an aperture/shutter-speed combination that best matches the information recorded by the light meter.

The caveat is that the camera's electronics can be fooled, resulting in a less than perfect picture. See the *Exposure Compensation* entry for more information on how to adjust programmed autoexposure to handle tricky lighting situations.

The bottom line is that programmed autoexposure is a reliable tool for capturing good pictures most of the time. You can increase your odds by learning a few of the override controls such as exposure compensation, spot metering, and exposure lock.

Protect Images

The Erase All command removes all images from your memory card. It's a handy way to clean house without having to remove each picture individually. What if, however, you wanted to remove all pictures except for one or two? The *Protect Images* option can help you do just that.

First, display the picture on the LCD monitor. Choose "Protect Images" from the menu, and an icon (such as a key) should appear on the monitor, to indicate that the picture is safe. Then you can use the Erase All command to delete the other images.

Be sure to practice this on test pictures to make sure everything works properly. Also, remember that Protect Images doesn't work when you use the Format Card command. All of your images will be erased, regardless of whether they are protected.

Resolution

By far one of the most important settings on your camera, *resolution* sets the pixel dimensions of your picture, thereby determining how big it can be displayed or printed later on. Most cameras allow you to set the resolution of the picture using a menu similar to the one in Figure 2-16.

If, for example, you select your camera's smallest pixel dimensions—say, 640×480—your picture will be adequate for web page display. But if you wanted to make a photo-quality print of that picture, then you would only have enough resolution for a 3×4" print at best.

On the other hand, if you had selected your camera's maximum resolution, such as 1600×1200 pixels (on a 2-megapixel camera), then you could make a 5×7" photo quality print, or even a good 8×10" print from the same picture. (See Table 7 in the Appendix for more details.)

The tradeoff is that the higher the resolution, the more room each picture occupies on your memory card. So, if you have a 2-megapixel camera with a 128MB memory card, you could squeeze 128 pictures on the card when the camera is set to its highest resolution (1600×1200 pixels). At medium resolution, 1024×768, your capacity increases to 271 pictures. And at the smallest resolution, 640×480, you can save a whopping 577 pictures to your card!

As tempting as 577 pictures sound, remember, if you take that once-in-a-lifetime shot at 640×480, your once-in-a-lifetime print will always be wallet size. On the other hand, if you shoot at 1600×1200, you have the option of making a nice 8×10" print, and if you just want to send images via email to friends and family, you can scale down your "master" image to a smaller resolution before mailing.

For more information on preparing your pictures for email, see Send Pictures Via Email in Chapter 3.

Figure 2-16. Resolution menu: generally speaking, the higher settings are on the left, and resolution declines as you move to settings on the right. The highest resolution setting for a 4-megapixel camera is shown here.

Self-Timer

The easiest way for you as the photographer to join a group shot is to use the camera's self-timer, which delays the triggering of the shutter (after you push the button) for 10 seconds or so. First, position the camera on a solid surface or on a tripod, then compose the picture. Before firing away, activate the self-timer. When you push the shutter button, the camera will count to 10 before taking the picture—giving you plenty of time to join your friends.

One of the tricks to self-timer mastery is to make sure the camera's focusing sensor is reading the subjects and not the background. Be especially careful when using the self-timer for portraits of couples, because the sensor often reads the area right between their heads. If your camera has *focus lock*, then you might want to use it. Using manual focus is also handy for these types of shots, but only advanced cameras offer this option. The self-timer can also be used

Figure 2-17. The self-timer is also a valuable tool for capturing colorful night shots. This evening composition of the San Francisco Museum of Modern Art was taken by placing the camera on a ledge and using the self-timer to trip the shutter. Even though the exposure was a lengthy half-second in duration, the picture is nice and sharp thanks to good technique.

as a substitute for a remote (or cable) release, which comes in handy for pictures that require the shutter to be open for a long time, such as a nighttime shot when the camera is on a tripod (See Figure 2-17). By using the self-timer or remote release, you can trip the shutter without vibrating the camera. Some cameras make this even easier by providing you with a 2-second option to complement the standard 10-second delay. That way you don't have to wait nearly as long for the shutter to trip once you've activated the timer.

Sequence Shooting

See *Burst/Continuous Shooting Mode*.

Shutter Priority

See *Timed Value (TV)*.

Spot Meter

This metering pattern enables you to "read" the exposure for a small area or "spot" in the viewfinder, usually 5 percent or less of the center of the frame. Not all cameras include a spot meter option, but those that do enable the photographer to set the exposure on an element in the composition rather than on the scene as a whole.

The most practical method for spot metering is to point the metering area at the object in the scene that is most important to you, then use exposure lock. Now recompose the scene any way you want, knowing that the most important element in the picture will be exposed properly.

Some cameras have *partial metering* instead of a true spot meter. Partial metering behaves the same way as a spot meter, but the metering area is bigger. Spot meters usually read 5 percent or less of the viewfinder, while partial metering patterns typically read about 10 percent.

Timed Value (TV)

Often referred to as *shutter priority*, this setting is commonly available on advanced consumer and pro-level cameras. TV enables you to set the shutter speed and lets the camera figure out the corresponding aperture setting. A common use for TV is sports photography, in which the action is frozen with a "fast" shutter speed.

But TV is also useful for situations that demand a very slow shutter speed, such as to create a soft, dreamlike effect with running water. Here are a few scenarios where you might want to switch to shutter priority mode:

Sports events. A fast shutter speed of 1/500th or 1/1000th of a second will "stop the action." You'll need plenty of ambient light to use these settings. In a pinch, you can increase your ISO speed setting to 400 to make your camera more light sensitive, but remember that you'll also gain "image noise" as part of the bargain.

Children playing outdoors. A fast shutter speed of 1/250th or 1/500th of a second will help you record children at play. If you feel like you're missing good shots because of shutter lag (delay from the moment you press the shutter to when the picture is actually recorded), try using focus lock to shorten lag time. You may also want to turn on the fill flash (see *Flash Modes*) and stay within 10 feet of your subjects. In addition to improving the lighting for outdoor portraits, flash helps freeze the action.

Running water. The effect you want will determine the shutter speed you choose. If you want to freeze the water and see droplets suspended in air, use a fast shutter speed such as 1/250 or 1/500. If you're shooting a waterfall and want a soft, dreamlike effect (see Figure 2-18), select a slow shutter speed such as 1/8. In this case, make sure you have your camera securely mounted on a tripod.

PRO TIP

If the scene is too bright for you to use a slow shutter speed, hold your sunglasses over the lens while making the exposure. Not only will this create a longer exposure, but you'll also get a nice polarizing effect as a bonus! If your camera accepts accessory filters, one of the best thing to have in your kit is a polarizer, which is much easier to use than holding sunglasses over the lens.

Streaking lights. To show motion, use a very slow shutter speed such as 2, 4, or even 8 seconds if your camera provides those options (this method is particularly effective at twilight with car lights as they drive by). Again, mounting your camera on a tripod is essential. If you have a remote release, you might want to use it to prevent you from jarring the camera as you trip the shutter.

These examples don't cover every situation, but they will help you use shutter priority to create the effect you want when working with subjects in motion.

Figure 2-18. By using a slow shutter speed, the photographer was able to soften the appearance of the falling water (exposure set to 1 second at f-8). A tripod and a bit of patience are necessary to capture this type of shot.

White Balance

Different light sources, such as tungsten light bulbs, produce light at different color temperatures than normal daylight (different temperatures often result in pictures that are "cooler" or "bluish" in some situations, or "warmer" or "reddish" in others). Your optical/nervous system compensates for these variations in color, but cameras need a little help as you move from outdoors to in. Film cameras rely on color correction filters to capture natural tones under a variety of conditions. Digital cameras make things easier by providing a built-in *white balance* adjustment. This control not only allows you to capture pictures with accurate tones, but also enables you to preview the effect on your LCD monitor before you take the shot. Think of the white balance control as your own personal filter collection built right into the camera.

The default setting for your camera is *auto white balance*. This mode works amazingly well most of the time. To test for yourself, point the camera at a different light source, such as a regular light bulb, and watch in the LCD monitor as the image slowly goes from very amber to a less surreal off-white.

But the effect produced by auto white balance may not always be exactly what you're looking for. In these instances, you can override the auto mode via one of the color correction presets available on your camera. Here's a list of the most common ones.

Daylight. Used for general outdoor photography. Adds slight warmth to the coloring to offset a blue cloudless sky.

Cloudy. Helps correct overcast skies, but is also good for shooting in open shade, such as under a tree. This setting adds more warmth to the scene than the daylight selection. See Figure 2-19.

Tungsten. Adds a bluish tone to offset the reddish cast created by standard light bulbs.

Fluorescent. Corrects for the greenish cast under warm-white or cool-white fluorescent tubes.

Fluorescent H. Helps balance the color for daylight fluorescent tubes.

Many intermediate to advanced cameras also include a custom white balance that allows the camera to find the right color correction when you point your camera at a white surface. Even better, some advanced digital SLRs, such as the Canon 10D, let you select specific hues via the Kelvin color temperature scale. If your camera has this capability, be sure to see Table 9 in the Appendix for a complete listing of Kelvin degrees and their corresponding light sources.

Although these settings are designed to help you create as natural color as possible, you can also use them creatively. For example, if you were shooting a portrait indoors next to an open window, you would choose the cloudy setting to produce more natural skin tones. But what if you wanted to convey a more somber mood? By using the "tungsten" setting, the ambient light transforms to a bluish-colored hue, changing the mood of the entire shot.

The white balance settings are both practical and creative tools for the digital photographer.

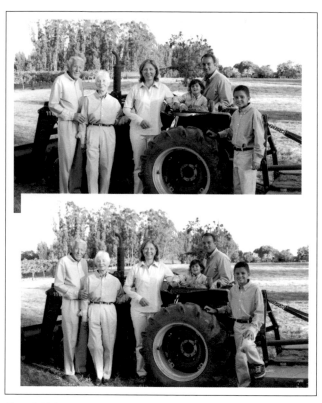

Figure 2-19. Warm up those cool tones. Both images were shot in open shade. The top photo was recorded with the white balance set to "Auto." Observe how cool the tones are, especially noticeable in the pants and skin. For the bottom image, the white balance was set to "Cloudy" to warm up the overall hue of the composition. Which is better? That's up to you, but understanding how to use white balance settings will give you more control.

Zoom/Magnify Control

Most people are familiar with using the zoom lever (or buttons) to zoom in and out when composing images in picture-taking mode. But magnifying the picture you just captured on the LCD monitor for closer inspection is equally valuable.

The problem with LCD monitors is that they are very small, colorful, and sharp. What's wrong with that? If you don't "zoom in" when you review your pictures on these little screens, you might be misled as to the quality of your shots. In other words, LCD monitors make your pictures look better than they really are.

By using the magnify control to zoom in on your subject's face as you review the picture, you can get a better idea of its true quality. A perfect example is checking for correct exposure on the LCD monitor after you've taken a portrait. Much to your dismay, after you've uploaded the image to your computer, you see that the subject's eyes were closed. If you had used the magnify control right after you had taken the shot, you might have seen the closed eyes and continued the shoot.

Obviously, you don't want to employ the magnify control after every shot you take, but before you let your subject leave, take a few moments to review a sampling of the images so you know you won't be disappointed after you get home and upload the pictures.

Pulling It All Together

By now you've committed everything you learned in this section to memory, right? Well, probably not. That's why this book is a pocket guide and not a desktop reference. Keep it in your camera bag, backpack, or back pocket so you can refer to it over and over again.

As you continue to get comfortable with this information, you'll begin to use many of these functions in combination with one another to achieve the effect you want. For example, you may use both the *white balance* and *exposure compensation* adjustments to create a dark, moody indoor portrait. Then the next day, use the fill *flash mode* and *aperture priority* to shoot stunning bridal portraits at a wedding.

One of the great digital photography advantages is that you can experiment with these settings, and it doesn't cost you a penny. Plus you get immediate feedback from your efforts.

In Chapter 3, you'll start putting your camera knowledge to work as you learn many of the techniques that pros use to create great images. So recharge those lithiums, and let's get to it.

How Do I...
Tips and Tricks for Shooting and Sharing

By now, you and your digital camera have become fast friends and are working together to make great images. But like the art of cooking, and life, there's always more to learn.

This chapter is more conversational than the previous two. The earlier sections of the book were designed for quick reference—to use while standing on the battlefield of photography and trying to survive. (Question: "Should I turn the flash on or off for my daughter's outdoor birthday party?" Answer: Flash on.)

But now the discussion becomes free flowing, like a conversation between two photographers trying to decide the best approach for a given situation. The topics in this chapter focus on both shooting and sharing pictures—what good is a great shot if you can't share it with others?

So grab a fresh memory card, a charged set of batteries, and prepare for the next stage of your journey.

Shooting Tips and Tricks— How Do I ...

How do I... ? Those are the first three words in any photography question, aren't they? Most of the time you know what you want to do: capture that sunset, take a pretty portrait, preserve the memory of that monument. The trick is making the camera see your subject the way you do.

That's what you're going to learn here: the "how to" of photography. Not every situation is covered in this chapter, but if you master these techniques, there won't be too many pictures that get by your camera. And when your friends mutter out loud something like, "How do I shoot that object inside the glass case?" you can reply, "Oh that's easy. Just put the edge of the lens barrel against the glass to minimize reflections, then turn off the flash."

Take Great Outdoor Portraits

When most folks think of portrait photography, they envision studio lighting, canvas backdrops, and a camera perched upon a tripod. But many photographers don't have access to lavish professional studios, and honestly, they're not necessary for dynamite portraits.

All you really need is a willing subject, a decent outdoor setting (preferably with trees), and your digital camera. Then you can be on your way to creating outstanding images.

First, start with the magic rules for great outdoor portraits:

Get close. The tighter you frame the shot, the more impact it will have. Extend your zoom lens and move your feet to create more powerful images. Once you've moved in close and have shot a series of images, get closer and shoot again.

Try adding supplemental light from the flash or a reflector. Turning on the flash outdoors is a trick that wedding photographers have been using for years. If you really want to impress your subjects, position them in the open shade (such as under a tree) with a nice background in the distance. Then turn on the fill flash and make sure you're standing within 10 feet (so the flash can reach the subject). The camera will balance the amount of light from the flash with the natural background illumination, resulting an evenly exposed portrait. (See Figure 2-1 on page 21 and Figure 2-11 on page 37 for examples of portraits using fill flash.) A variation on this technique is to turn off the flash and use a reflector to "bounce" the light back toward the model's face. The advantage here is that the reflected light is softer than that from a fill flash (see Figure 3-1).

Learn to love high clouds and overcast days. High clouds turn the entire sky into a giant lighting softbox, and all of nature becomes your portrait studio. The diffused lighting is perfect for outdoor portraits. In this situation, you have the option of shooting without flash and reflectors. Or, if you want to add a little "kick," you can turn on the fill flash. Figure 3-2 was shot on an overcast morning with no fill flash. Notice how the diffused lighting softens the skin tones. If you want to brighten up the eyes a bit, turn on the fill flash or use a reflector. One thing to remember when shooting in this type of lighting: change your white balance to "cloudy," or the skin tones will be too cool.

Once you've found a setting that you like and have everything in order, you can "work the scene."

Start by taking a few straightforward images. Pay close attention while you have the model turn a little to the left, then to the right. When you see a position you like, shoot a few

Figure 3-1. Open shade portrait. By putting the subject in the shade, you can control the lighting. For this shot, a reflector was positioned on the photographer's left to bounce light back to the shadow areas. Fill flash can be used instead if you prefer. (Program mode, 1/125 at f-4.)

frames. (Don't get too carried away with this "working the angles thing," or people will hate you. You're not a swimsuit photographer on a *Sports Illustrated* location shoot. But the point is, don't be afraid to experiment with different camera positions. Just do it quickly.)

Figure 3-2. Overcast days are perfect for portraits. This image was recorded with only the light from the diffused sky. The white balance was set to "cloudy" to warm up the skin tones. (Program mode, 1/90 at f-5.6.)

Next, move in closer and work a few more angles. Raise the camera and have the model look upward; lower the camera and have the subject look away. Be sure to take lots of shots while experimenting with angles, because once you're finished shooting and review the images later on your computer screen, you'll discard many of those images that looked great on the camera's LCD monitor. The problem is that when they're enlarged, you'll see bothersome imperfections you didn't notice before.

Communicate with your subjects and try to put them at ease. Nobody likes the silent treatment from the photographer. It makes them feel like you're unhappy with how the shoot is going.

Here are a few more things to avoid when shooting outdoor portraits.

Avoid harsh side-lighting on faces. Light coming in from the side accentuates texture. That's the last thing most models want to see in their shots because texture equates to skin aging or imperfections. Use a fill flash or reflector to minimize texture and avoid side lighting unless for special effect.

Don't show frustration. Never, ever make subjects feel it's their fault that the shoot isn't going well. They're already putting their self-confidence on the line by letting you take their picture. Don't make them regret that decision. When shots go well, credit goes to the model. When shots go badly, it's the photographer's fault. Keep your ego in check so theirs can stay intact.

Avoid skimping on time or the number of frames you shoot. Your images may look good on that little 2" LCD monitor, but when you blow them up on the computer screen, you're going to see lots of things you don't like. Take many shots of each pose and, if you're lucky, you'll end up with a few you really like.

Don't torture models by making them look into the sun. Yes, you were told for years to shoot with the sun to your back. The photographer, not the model, devised that rule. Blasting your subjects' retinas with direct sun is only going to make them squint, sweat, and maybe swear. Be kind to your models and they'll reward you with great shots.

Avoid busy backgrounds. Bright colors, linear patterns, and chaotic landscape elements will detract from your compositions. Look for continuous tones without the hum of distracting elements.

Now that the basics are covered, here are a couple of super Pro Tips. These aren't techniques that you should use until you have good, solid shots recorded on your memory card. But once you do, maybe try these suggestions.

Soft background portraits. These are simply lovely. A soft, slightly out-of-focus background keeps the viewer's eye on the model and gives your shots a real professional look. The mechanics of this technique are described in Chapter 2 under Aperture Priority with an example illustrated in Figure 2-1 on page 21.

Rim lighting for portraits. When you place the sun behind the model, often you get highlights along the hair. Certain hairstyles really accentuate this effect. Remember to use fill flash for this setup or your model's face will be underexposed. Rim lighting was used for Figure 2-11 on page 37.

Set Up Group Shots

Many of the rules for engaging portraits apply to group shots too. So keep in mind everything that you've learned so far while preparing for this assignment.

The first challenge is to arrange the group into a decent composition. If you've ever participated in a wedding, you know this drill. Figure 3-3 shows a classic triangle composition for three people.

Remind everyone in the shot that they need to have a clear view of the camera. If they can't see the camera, the camera can't see them. Next, position people as close together as possible. Group-shot participants tend to stand too far apart. That might look okay in real life, but the camera accentuates the distance between people and the result looks awkward. Plus,

Figure 3-3. The classic "triangle" composition is effective for a three-person group shot. Notice that distracting background elements are kept to a minimum. The subjects are positioned in the shade to eliminate harsh shadows on the face and squinty eyes. A fill flash is used for even front illumination. (Program mode, 1/60 at f-5.6.)

you can't afford to have this shot span as wide as a football field, or you'll never see people's faces unless you enlarge the image to poster size.

Remember to take lots of shots—for large groups, a minimum of five frames. This gives you a chance to overcome blinking eyes, sudden head turns, bad smiles, and unexpected gusts of wind ruining your pictures.

PRO TIP

Carry a stepladder for big group shots. When shooting groups of 10 or more, it's best to find steps so you can stagger their heights and compose a more compact shot. But if steps aren't available, you can climb a few rungs on a portable ladder. By elevating the camera, you have a better chance to capture a clean shot of everyone's face.

How Do I...

Before pressing the shutter button, quickly scan the group looking for little annoyances that will drive you crazy later: crooked ties, sloppy hair, and turned-up collars will make you insane during postproduction.

Finally, work quickly. You're not John Ford making the great American epic, so don't act like it. Keep things moving for the sake of your subjects. (And for your own tired feet!)

Capture Existing-Light Portraits

By now you've probably realized one of the great ironies in good portrait photography: the flash is your friend when working outdoors. So guess what the great secret is for indoor portraiture? That's right; sometimes it's better to turn the flash off. Some of the most artistic portraits use nothing more than an open window and a simple reflector.

The problem with using your on-camera flash indoors is that the light is harsh and creates an image filled with contrast. "Harsh" and "high contrast" are two words models don't like to hear when it comes to picture descriptions.

Fill flash works outdoors because everything is bright. The flash "fills" right in. But ambient light is much dimmer indoors, and the burst of light from the flash is much like a car approaching on a dark street.

Of course there are times when you have no choice but to use your camera's flash indoors. It's very convenient, and you do get a recognizable picture. But when you have the luxury of setting up an artistic portrait in a window-lit room, try existing light only.

First, position the model near an open window and study the scene. You can't depend solely on your visual perception, because your eyes and brain are going to read the lighting a little differently than the camera will, especially in the shadow areas—you will see detail in the dark areas that the camera can't record.

This is why you'll probably want to use a reflector to "bounce" some light into the shadow areas. Many photographers swear by collapsible light discs, but a large piece of white cardboard or foam core will work just as well. Place your reflector opposite the window and use it to "bounce" the light onto the dark side of the model. This will help "fill in" the shadow area so you can see some detail.

Now put your camera on a tripod and slowly squeeze the shutter button. Review the image on the LCD monitor. If the shadow area is too dark, you may want to add another reflector. If the overall image is too dark, turn on exposure compensation, set it to +1, and try another picture. If the color balance of the image is too cool (bluish), you may want to set the white balance control to "cloudy" and see if that improves the rendering.

Remind your model to sit very still during exposure because you may be using a shutter speed that's as slow as 1/15th of a second or longer. You could increase the camera's light sensitivity by adjusting the ISO speed to 200, but don't go beyond that setting—the image quality will degrade too much for this type of shot.

Once you've played with these variables, go back to the artistic side of your brain and work on the composition. Try to get all the elements in the picture working together and let nature's sweet light take it from there. When it all comes together, existing-light portraits are magical. (See Figure 3-4).

Shoot Good Self-Portraits

Some people may think that turning the camera toward oneself is the height of narcissism, but sometimes you need a shot, and no one is around to take it for you. These are the times when it's good to know how to shoot a self-portrait.

Start with the basics: make sure your hair is combed, collar is down, shirt is clean, and your teeth are free from spinach (and lipstick!).

Figure 3-4. Three lighting options for indoor portraits. Sometimes you just have to use fill flash, as in the top left image; this lighting tends to be harsh and often casts a shadow on the background. Window illumination is much softer, but highly directional from one angle, as in the right image—notice the deep shadow on the side of the face away from the light source. By placing a reflector opposite the window directed back at the subject, as in the bottom left image, you can lighten the shadows, creating a more evenly illuminated portrait.

Then find a location with a pleasing, uncluttered background. Put the camera on a tripod and set it to focus on the area where you'll be standing or sitting. Activate the self-timer.

If the room is too dim for an existing-light portrait, try using "slow-synchro" flash (see Flash Modes in Chapter 2 for more information). This type of flash provides enough illumination for a good portrait, but slows down the shutter enough to record the ambient light in the room.

Now position yourself where you had focused the camera and look directly into the lens. Don't forget to smile.

Take several shots, trying different poses until you hit on a few you like. If you have a remote release for your camera, you can save yourself lots of running back and forth from the tripod to the modeling position.

PRO TIP

Position a mirror behind the camera so you can better pose yourself at the moment of exposure.

Self-portraits are perfect for experimenting with different "looks" that might have made you self-conscious with someone else behind the camera. You can try different expressions and poses, erase the bad ones, and the world will never know the difference.

Take Interesting Kid Shots

Children are a challenge for consumer digital cameras, primarily because of shutter lag. In short, kids move faster than digicams can react. But with a few adjustments, you can capture excellent images that you'll cherish for years.

One of the most important adjustments, regardless of the type of camera you're using, is to get down to kid level when shooting. This is "hands and knees" photography at its best, as shown in Figure 3-5. And if you need to, get on your belly for just the right angle. By doing so, your shots will instantly become more engaging.

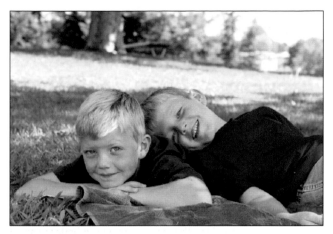

Figure 3-5. Go where the kids are to get good shots. Don't be afraid to get down on the ground. And once you're there, you might want to turn on the fill flash to help you stop action and evenly illuminate the portrait. (Program mode, 1/90 at f-5.6 with the flash on.)

Next, get close. Then get closer. This may seem impossible at times with subjects who move so fast, but if you want great shots, then you've got to keep your subjects within range.

Now turn on the flash, regardless of whether you're indoors or out. Not only will this provide even illumination, but flash helps "freeze" action, and you'll need all the help you can get in this category.

Finally, use the "focus lock" technique described in the practical example Capturing the Decisive Moment in Chapter 2. By doing so, you can reduce shutter lag and increase your percentage of good shots.

Some of the most rewarding pictures you'll ever record will be of children. Like the child-rearing process itself, kid photography requires patience. But the results can far surpass the effort.

Capture Engaging Travel Locations

Make sure you pack a spare memory card and extra batteries when you hit the road with your digital camera, as these compact picture-takers are perfect travel companions.

When you're on the road, approach your travel photography the same way a director thinks about filming a movie scene. The first frame, often called the *establishing shot*, is of the point of interest itself, such as an old church. The second image is a nicely framed portrait with an *element of the structure* included in the picture. If the subject warrants it, you might even want to move in very close for a third shot.

Why multiple shots? For the same reason that moviemakers use this technique. If you try to tell the whole story with just establishing shots, your viewers may soon lose interest in the presentation. That's the problem with so many vacation shots—they're taken at too great a distance. See Figure 3-6.

Figure 3-6. The juxtaposition of old and new is quite striking while taking a walk in San Francisco, CA. This establishing shot gives the viewer a sense of the area. (Aperture priority, 1/250 at f-5.6.)

On the other hand, if you make all of your travel compositions tightly framed only, your viewers won't know the difference between Denmark and Detroit. By using the multiple-shot approach, you establish both the setting and the detail of each location. This method is particularly effective when building slideshows. See Figures 3-7 and 3-8.

Figure 3-7. By zooming in closer for a tighter composition, you can provide more detail information. (Aperture priority, 1/250 at f-5.6.)

Figure 3-8. If the subject warrants more attention, you might want to observe it from different angles and zoom in even tighter. (Aperture priority, 1/50 at f-2-5.)

PRO TIP

Don't forget to take pictures of signs and placards. It's a lot easier than taking notes, and the information comes in very handy when recounting your travel experiences.

Take Pictures at Weddings

Weddings are portrait heaven. Your subjects look sharp, are happy, and are in pretty settings. All you have to do have your camera ready for the opportunities as they present themselves.

1. Rule one is to not interfere with the hired photographer's shots. If you want "follow in his wake" for special posed portraits, simply ask permission to shoot a couple frames after he finishes. Most pros will accommodate these polite requests.

2. Next, turn on your flash and leave it on—indoors or out. See Flash Modes in Chapter 2 for an overview of your options and how to use them.

3. When you're taking group shots, remember to position guests as closely as possible. Generally speaking, people stand too far apart. Get them close together.

4. Make sure everyone in the group has a clear view of the camera. If they can't see the camera, then the camera can't see them. If you have to, stand on a stable chair to get a better angle for group shots. The choice for large groups is simple: either vary the heights of those in the group by using steps or risers, or raise the camera angle above their heads and shoot downward.

5. Keep an eye out for candids too, as shown in Figure 3-9. Look for those special moments that make these gatherings so memorable—a kiss on the cheek, a sleepy child in a guest's arms, the perfect toast, a romantic dance sequence, or guests signing—these are all potential great photographs just waiting for you to shoot.

Finally, don't forget to include props in the shots when available. A hint of wedding cake in the background or a beautiful flower arrangement could be the frosting that adds the perfect finish to your portrait. Figure 3-10 also demonstrates how personal touches can help.

Figure 3-9. Even if you're not the hired photographer, there are plenty of opportunities for pleasing images at a wedding. Just follow the action and have your camera ready. (Program mode, 1/60 at f-2.5 with the flash on.)

Figure 3-10. Keep your eyes peeled for the personal touches that make this event different than others. Chances are the bride and groom spent a great deal of time planning the details. When you recognize and capture them, those pictures are sure to please the new couple. (Program mode, 1/60 at f-5.6, flash on.)

Prevent Red Eye

Your subjects are vulnerable to red eye in dimly lit rooms when their pupils are open wide. The effect is actually caused by the light from the flash bouncing off the retina and reflected back into the picture-taking lens. Point-and-shoot cameras are notorious for causing red eye because the flash is so close to the lens, making for a perfect alignment to catch the reflection from the retina.

Even though many cameras provide a setting to reduce red eye (see Flash Modes in Chapter 2), they don't always work well and actually can be irritating to both subject and photographer. Instead, try to incorporate as many of these tips as possible when shooting in low light:

- Have the model look directly at a light source, such as a lamp, before taking the shot. This will constrict the pupils and reduce red eye.

- Turn up the room lights if possible.

- Shoot off to the side of the subject, or have the model look a little to the left or the right of the camera, but not directly at the lens.

- Use an external flash mounted on a bracket. This is how wedding photographers cope with this problem. It works by changing the angle of reflection from the retina.

- Try an existing-light portrait if conditions are suitable.

If all else fails, you can touch up the photograph in an image editor after uploading. It's not a perfect solution, but easier than it used to be, thanks to friendlier computer technology (for help with touching up red eye, try *iPhoto 2: The Missing Manual* or *Photoshop Elements 2: The Missing Manual*, both from Pogue Press).

Take Pictures from the Stands of Sporting Events

Speaking of flash, how many times have you seen hundreds of cameras firing off from the stands during a sporting event in a large stadium? Alas, what a waste of film.

The flash distance for most point-and-shoot cameras is about 10 feet. That means if you're shooting from the stands, you're illuminating a couple rows of seats in front of you, and that's about it. Instead, *turn off your flash* and use existing-light techniques. If you can adjust your camera's ISO setting (see ISO Speed in Chapter 2), then bump it up to 200 or 400. This will increase your camera's light sensitivity.

When you take the shot, hold the camera very steady because the shutter speed will be slow, and you'll want to minimize *camera shake*, which degrades image quality. Better yet, use a tripod if the situation allows.

Even if you hold the camera steady, the action on the playing field will blur, so try to make your exposures right after, or before, the action.

Obviously you're not going to get *Sports Illustrated* shots from the cheap seats. But for memorable occasions, such as Barry Bonds hitting his 600th home run, it's great to have a few well-exposed images from the event to keep in the scrapbook.

Capture Action Shots

The four keys to capturing effective action shots are to shoot at your camera's highest resolution, use a fast shutter speed, take measures to reduce shutter lag, and use burst mode with infinity lock. See Figure 3-11.

1. First, set your camera at its highest resolution. You will probably want to "crop in" your image later to bring the action closer. Having extra pixels actually extends the reach of your lens, which is very helpful for this type of photography.

Figure 3-11. Two of the most important techniques for stopping action and capturing the decisive moment are to use a fast shutter speed (1/350 for this shot) and enable "burst mode," which allows you to fire off a rapid series of frames. Then pick the best image from the sequence.

2. The key to "stopping action" is to use a fast shutter speed setting. Typically, you should use a speed of at least 1/250th, 1/500th, or 1/1000th of a second. The programmed autoexposure mode on most digital cameras is calibrated to give you the fastest shutter speed possible, so you don't need to monkey too much with your camera settings when going after action shots.

3. But what you really need is lots of light. The brightest hours of the day are best, usually from 9:00 a.m to 4:00 p.m. Shooting during these times outdoors should produce shutter speeds of 1/250th of a second or faster. If you have shutter priority mode, you can set the speed yourself and let the camera handle the corresponding aperture setting.

4. Unfortunately, a fast shutter speed doesn't help you overcome the lag time between the moment you press the picture-taking button and when the shutter actually fires. *Shutter lag* is the nemesis of digital action photographers,

and overall, it's the number one complaint about consumer digicams. Most digital cameras have two features that can help you combat shutter lag.

- The first is *burst mode*, which allows you to take a rapid sequence of shots. If you start the sequence right as the action is initiated, your odds of capturing the decisive moment are much higher. (See Burst/Continuous Shooting Mode in Chapter 2.)

- The other trick is to "preset the focus," thereby disabling the auto focus system and shortening the lag time between pressing the picture-taking button and actually recording the picture. The best way to do this is to use a function called *infinity lock*. The camera "locks in" the focus at infinity, which provides you a range from about 10 feet to forever. Once infinity lock is engaged, you can fire at will without relying on the auto focus system. Sometimes you have to switch to "Landscape mode" in order to activate the infinity lock. This doesn't seem intuitive, but often it works. For more information on this function, see the Infinity Lock section in Chapter 2.

PRO TIP

If there's not enough light to use a fast shutter speed to stop the action, increase your ISO setting to 200 or 400. You'll gain a little image noise in the bargain, but it might be worth the tradeoff to get a better shot.

Another helpful technique for action shooting is called *panning*, in which you "follow" the moving subject during exposure. Using this technique may feel odd at first, because you're taught to always hold the camera as still as possible when taking the picture. But panning can provide stunning results; if you follow the subject accurately, it will be in focus while the background displays motion blur. This effect gives the photograph great energy and a sense of movement.

The classic panning exercise is to have a bicyclist ride by while you keep the camera fixed on the rider during exposure. Use focus lock and burst mode to give yourself the best odds for timing the shot correctly. You might not be able to fully appreciate the effect on your small LCD monitor, but when you upload the images to your computer you'll see this wonderfully blurred background providing the sensation of motion. Give it a try!

Shoot in Museums

Museums, aquariums, and natural-habitat parks provide opportunities for unusual shots. They also present some difficult challenges for the digital photographer, but nothing that can't be overcome with a little ingenuity.

Before you get too excited at the prospects of shooting beautiful works of art in a museum, be sure to ask if it's okay. Often you'll discover that photography is allowed in some areas, but not in others. To avoid embarrassing confrontations, ask when you first enter the facility.

Even when you're granted permission, you'll probably be told that you can't use a flash or set up a tripod. So here are a few tips to help you work around those constraints.

1. Check your *white balance*. Chances are your images are displaying a noticeable reddish hue in your LCD monitor. Try using the "Tungsten" setting to improve the color balance. Some cameras allow you to set a custom color balance. You might want to give that a try if the presets don't provide the results you want. For more information, see White Balance in Chapter 2.

2. Find a way to combat the low ambient light often found inside museums. Chances are the *camera shake* symbol is

flashing on your LCD monitor telling you that your pictures are going to be "soft" due to a slow shutter speed.

3. If your camera has a neck strap, you can use it to help you steady the shots. Pull the camera out from your body until the strap is taut. Use this resistance to steady your hands as you make the exposure. If available, you can also lean against a wall or pillar to help you combat camera shake.

4. As a last resort, you can increase your camera's light sensitivity by adjusting the ISO setting. Changing the setting to 200 or 400 might get rid of the camera shake warning, but your picture quality won't be as good. For more information, see ISO Speed in Chapter 2.

Regardless of the type of museum you're visiting, you're probably going to encounter glass cases and exhibits behind glass, such as the one in Figure 3-12. The trick to eliminating unwanted reflections is to put the outer edge of the camera's lens barrel right up against the glass, hold the camera steady, then shoot. By putting the lens barrel close to the glass, you eliminate those nasty room reflections that often ruin otherwise beautiful shots.

PRO TIP

Unwanted reflections often appear in your pictures when you're shooting through exhibit glass. The image of a moon jellyfish was shot through aquarium glass, but the edge of the camera's lens barrel was gently placed directly on the glass of the exhibit, thereby eliminating unwanted reflections (Figure 3-12). Because the ambient light was low, the ISO setting had to be increased to 400 in order to increase the camera's sensitivity. Remember, you have to

---

Once you upload your pictures from your visit to the museum, you'll probably notice that many of the images suffer from softness and other maladies that you didn't detect in the LCD

Figure 3-12. Moon jellyfish through glass aquarium. Notice that you can see some "image noise" in this picture due to pushing the ISO setting to 400. In this case, the ability to capture the image in low light was worth the tradeoff of a little image noise. (Aperture priority, 1/30 at f-2, flash off.)

monitor. Don't despair, though—even if only a fraction of your images survive, they'll be treasured for years to come, and are well worth the effort of capturing.

Shoot Architecture Like a Pro

Adding pictures of buildings and their interesting elements to your travel pictures brings another dimension to your presentations. Point-and-shoot cameras aren't ideal for architectural shooting, but by following these suggestions, you'll be surprised by the results you can achieve.

You may have noticed a phenomenon called *converging lines* when taking pictures of large buildings. Instead of the structure standing straight and tall, it looks distorted. This effect occurs because the plane of the camera isn't parallel to the plane of the building. The problem of non-parallel planes is caused by your having to shoot upward at the tall structure (the building is standing at a 90-degree angle, and your camera is most likely angled 45 degrees or so). By angling your camera upward to frame the shot, you create distortion because the planes of the camera and the building are not parallel.

One trick is to elevate your height so your can point the camera straight at the building instead of upward (so both camera and building are angled at 90 degrees). Maybe you can go over to a building across the way and shoot through an open window from the second or third floor. Look for positions that allow you to shoot "across" instead of "upward" if you want to eliminate distortion (see Figure 3-13).

But don't limit yourself to shooting only the big picture: architectural elements are often just as interesting (if not more so) than the complete structure. And the best part is that distortion is much easier to control with smaller elements than with the entire building.

Figure 3-13. Tall buildings standing straight because the plane of the camera is parallel to the plane of the structures. In this case, the picture was taken from the seventh floor of a hotel across the way. (Aperture priority, 1 second at f-2.)

Look for interesting designs around windows, over doors, and along the roofline. Zoom in on specific areas that interest you, or elements that you might have missed during casual observation (see Figure 3-14).

To enhance textures and depth, look for "side lighting" that often provides more interesting images than flat front lighting. And don't forget to grab a couple snaps of signs and placards to help you tell the story once you return home.

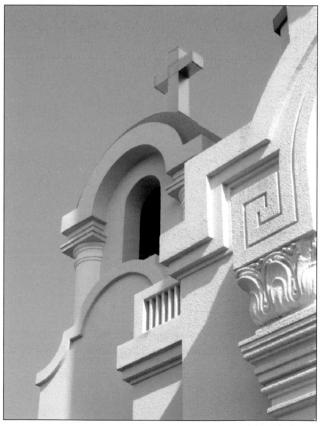

Figure 3-14. Church shot in morning side lighting. (Aperture priority, 1/640 at f-3.5.)

PRO TIP

Side lighting is good for buildings because it enhances texture, but not so good for people, for the same reason.

Shoot Items Using Tabletop Photography

There are two ways to shoot items using tabletop photography: the hard way and the easy way. The hard way involves multiple studio lights, soft boxes, umbrellas, and seamless backdrop paper. Professionals use this equipment to produce outstanding images for commercial advertising and high-end editorial work.

But if you just want a nice picture of your old 35mm camera to sell on eBay, you probably don't want to set up an entire studio. So here's the easy way:

1. Find a window that you can set a table next to. North-facing windows are great, but not necessary for this type of shooting. Cover the surface with white paper, and if you can, create a white backdrop too. This will be your work area.

2. Put your camera on a tripod and adjust it so it's facing the item that you want to photograph on the table. Move both the subject and the camera to achieve the best lighting possible via the open window. Once everything is in place, make a tabletop reflector out of white cardboard or cover a card with aluminum foil. Position the reflector opposite the light source (window) so it's bouncing light on to the shadow side of the item.

3. Adjust your white balance to "cloudy" (see White Balance in Chapter 2 for more information) and put your camera on self-timer (see Self-Timer in Chapter 2). Now trip the timer and stand back. After 10 seconds or so, the camera will take the shot for you to review. Continue refining your setup until you get the shot you want.

This simple setup can produce studio-like results at a fraction of the cost or effort. Give it a try.

Create Powerful Landscape Images

You could spend your entire lifetime studying how to make great landscape images. There are, however, a few key techniques that will improve your nature shots right away while you learn the subtleties of the craft. Keep these few tips (demonstrated in Figure 3-15) in the back of your mind while shooting.

Work with magic light. Landscape pictures shot *before* 9:00 a.m. and *after* 5.00 p.m. look better, especially with digital cameras that have a hard time taming harsh mid-day sun.

Keep your compositions simple. Clutter is the bane of landscape imagery. Look for simple, powerful compositions, and skip the rest.

Don't put the horizon line in the middle of the frame. Landscapes become more powerful when the horizon line is in the lower or upper third of the composition. You can create a very dynamic composition by putting the horizon very low in the frame and letting sky dominate the scene.

Look for converging lines to give the eye a path to follow. A diagonal line adds energy to the composition and can help lead the eye to a primary point of interest.

Alternate dark and light tones. This is a technique that Ansel Adams used quite effectively. He would find a dark tone for the bottom of the frame, then a light tone, then another dark area (usually a shadow of some sort), then bright again, and possibly dark at the top of the frame. Alternating tones add plenty of visual interest.

Figure 3-15. This image employs a few helpful landscape techniques. First, the horizon line is low in the frame, allowing for a "big sky." There are alternating dark and light tones for visual interest. The image was recorded in late afternoon, taking advantage of "magic light." Finally, the picture was shot at high resolution, allowing for some cropping to fine-tune the composition. (Aperture priority, 1/250 at f-8.)

Use a tripod when possible. By keeping your camera rock-steady, you will squeeze every bit of sharpness out of the lens, rendering even the tiniest elements with clarity. Plus, photographers who use tripods tend to study their scenes more and have more refined compositions.

Be patient. Sometimes you have to wait for nature to paint you the perfect picture. Allow enough time to stay put for a while and watch the light change.

Use a polarizing filter. If your camera accepts accessories such as auxiliary lens and filters, consider adding a polarizing filter to your bag of tricks. Polarizers remove unwanted reflections, deepen color saturation, and bring an overall clarity to the scene. The effect is strongest when the sunlight is shining onto the scene from over your shoulder.

Protect against lens flare by shielding the front glass element of your camera from the sun. Lens flare is that demon that degrades the color saturation of your images. Lens hoods were once standard issue for 35mm cameras, but no one seems to use them for digitals. To improve the quality of your shots, make sure the sun is not reflecting off the front of your lens. If it is, shield it with your hand, or better yet, this book, which is the perfect size for the job.

Shoot at the highest resolution and sharpness your camera allows. Landscapes look best when printed big. But to do so, you need all the resolution your camera can muster.

Get out and walk. If you see a good shot from the seat of your car, chances are it's even better a few hundred yards away from the road.

Don't increase your ISO speed setting to cope with low light. Bumping your speed will degrade the quality of your image. Use a tripod and your self-timer instead.

By keeping these tips in mind, and by reviewing the section Composition in Chapter 2, you can begin learning the craft of landscape photography with your digital point-and-shoot camera, and take some great shots while doing so.

Shoot Infrared Images

Infrared photography has been around for a long time, but capturing these stunning pictures on film required true perseverance. Digital imaging has changed all of that. Shooting infrared photos, such as the one shown in Figure 3-16, has never been easier or more fun.

Figure 3-16. This infrared image was captured midday in Sedona, AZ using a Canon G1 with a Hoya R72 filter attached. Because the filter is so dense, the shutter speed was a slow 1/3 of a second.

When you shoot infrared, you're dealing with a spectrum of light that's outside our normal range of perception. But with the assistance of a special filter, such as an IR 87 or Hoya R72, many digital cameras can produce the telltale dramatic effects, including a darkened sky, vivid clouds, and foliage emitting an eerie glow.

But not all digital cameras see the infrared spectrum equally. The irony is that as manufacturers made improvements in color fidelity, they often compromised the infrared capability.

For example, the older Canon G1 records fantastic infrared, but the following model, the G2, doesn't do so quite as well. (This is a good argument for holding on to your previous cameras after upgrading.)

If you want to test your digicams to see which one works the best for this type of shooting, line them up on a table in a darkened room. Enable picture-taking mode and make sure the LCD monitor is on. Then point your television remote control at each lens and press a control button, such as the channel changer. The camera that shows the brightest light emitting from the remote control will be your best infrared capture device.

Attach an infrared filter such as the Hoya R72 to your camera, grab your tripod, and look for a brightly lit scene that has sky, clouds, and trees. Set your aperture at f-11 or f-16 to help compensate for the different way infrared "sees" the world; the focusing plane in this type of photography is slightly different, and the added depth of field produced by a small aperture will help keep things sharp. Be sure to turn on the self-timer so you don't jar the camera during exposure, and record a frame.

PRO TIP

If you shoot your infrared images in color, you can later create some interesting effects on the computer by converting selected areas to black and white and leaving others in color. You'll need a good image editor such as Photoshop Elements to achieve this look.

The world you see in your LCD monitor will look much different from what you observe with your eyes. Record your infrared images in color, then, if you want, convert them to black and white later on the computer. That way you'll have more options for your finished product.

Take Flash Pictures of People Who Blink at Flash

Every now and then you'll run into someone whose eyes are very sensitive to flash and who has a knack for blinking right as the flash fires. The result is a series of unflattering facial expressions and lots of frustration.

One of the best tricks to help calm the nerves of model and photographer alike is to use the red-eye reduction mode. (See Flash Modes in Chapter 2 and Prevent Red Eye earlier in this chapter for more information.) The pre-flash that is designed to reduce red eye will actually cause the model to blink early, and their eyes will be open when the exposure takes place. It works almost every time.

Computer Tips and Tricks: How Do I …

You've just returned from a great two-week vacation and your memory cards are bursting at the seams. Now what do you do?

Before you spam everyone you know with triple-megapixel masters, take a few minutes to learn about *sampling down* images so they have smaller file sizes. You'll also want to archive your pictures so you can find them again months later when you want to relive the great memories.

In other words, this section will help you keep your friends happy and your pictures safe and sound.

Send Pictures Via Email

One of the things that new digital camera owners love to do is send batches of images to family members or friends. As you may have already discovered, the warmth of reception is inversely proportional to the size of the images that land in their inbox.

All too often, budding photographers send full-sized 1-, 2-, or even 3-megapixel pictures as email attachments. Unfortunately, these files take forever to download and are too large to view comfortably on a computer monitor.

Indeed, you should shoot at your camera's highest resolution, but remember not to send those full-sized images to others. All parties concerned will be much happier if you create smaller "email versions" of your pictures and send those along instead.

1. Use your image editor to resize a copy for easier handling. To do so, use the "Save As…" command in your image editor. The largest size you should send as an email attachment is 640×480 pixels, and 320×240 pixels will usually do the job.

2. If you're lucky enough to have Photoshop (or Photoshop Elements) as your image editor, use the Image Size function (see Figure 3-17) to resize the picture. (Other image editors have similar functions too.) When you first open the Image Size dialog box, you'll see the current width and height of the picture. In the settings in Figure 3-17, those dimensions are 2272 pixels wide by 1704 pixels tall. This shot was taken at full resolution with a 4-megapixel camera. If you sent this picture as-is, the file size would be well over 1 megabyte even after compression, and a full 11 megabytes when opened. That's not the kind of attachment you want to send to friends and family.

3. After using Image Size to reduce the pixel dimensions to 320×240 (as shown in Figure 3-18), the compressed file size shrank to under 100 kb—that's less than 1/10 the size of the original image!

4. Make sure you have both the "Constrain Proportions" and "Resample Image" boxes checked when preparing image copies for email. With the "Constrain Proportions" box checked, Photoshop will automatically change the height dimension for you.

Figure 3-17. The Image Size dialog box in Photoshop 7.

Figure 3-18. More appropriate dimensions for emailing pictures.

If you have a choice, the best image format to use for email attachments is JPEG (.jpg). When saving in this format, you will usually be asked (by your computer) which level of compression you want to use. Generally speaking, *medium* or *high* gives you the quality you need.

Remember to keep your original image safe and sound so you can use it later for printing and large display. To help eliminate confusion when dealing with these different sizes, you might want to save two copies, calling one *vacation one hires.jpg* and the more compact version *vacation one lores.jpg*.

By sending friends and family smaller, more manageable pictures, you'll hear more about how beautiful your shots are and less about how long the darn thing took to download.

PRO TIP

"Resampling" is probably one of those words you've heard before, but you're not quite sure what it means. In simplest terms, resampling means that the image editor is either adding or subtracting pixels to the image. Usually you want to avoid "sampling up," that is, adding pixels, because that degrades image quality. But "sampling down," or subtracting pixels, is a great way to reduce the file size of image copies that you want to send via email or post on the Web. In other words, when you change the width and height dimensions to smaller numbers, such as 320x240, you're sampling down, and both the picture and the file size will be smaller.

Get Photo-Quality Prints

There are a variety of ways to get photo-quality prints from your digital images. You can do them yourself with an inkjet printer, or have a photo finisher do the work for you.

Many camera stores offer photo finishing from digital images. Simply take in your memory card, order your prints, and pick them up the next day.

You can also order prints through online services such as Shutterfly (*http://www.shutterfly.com*). You have to upload your pictures via the Internet to their facility; they send you your prints back through the mail.

Either camera-store or online services make the most sense for photographers with busy schedules. On occasion, you may want to run a few pictures through the inkjet printer at home, but generally speaking, professional services are more convenient, and the resulting prints are of higher quality.

Present a Digital Slideshow

Presenting slideshows on a given subject is an age-old photographic tradition. Digital cameras make it easier than ever to present your images to many people at once.

Many digicams have a "video-out" capability that lets you connect your camera directly to a television for playback on a large screen. If your camera has this functionality, then it most likely has a slideshow mode that allows you to choose images that are stored on the memory card and present them on the television in timed intervals. All you have to do is turn on the stereo for some background music, add a little witty commentary, and you have a full-fledged multimedia presentation to share with others.

Another option is to use the software that comes with your camera to assemble slideshows on the computer, then either show them on the computer monitor or connect the computer to a television for big-screen presentations.

Computer slideshows have the advantage of being able to add transitions and special effects to the presentation. They can also be saved and played long after the memory card has been erased and reused.

You can also use independent software that didn't come with your camera for this purpose. Apple Computer's iPhoto not only enables you to make slideshows from your digital images, but also allows you to incorporate music directly into the presentation. You can even save the show as a QuickTime movie and send it to others.

Regardless of which method you use to create your presentations, keep in mind these basic tips that will help make your shows engaging and leave your audience begging for more.

- Include only your best images.

- Tell a story with your pictures as well as with your words.

- Keep your presentations short. Five to ten minutes is all the time that's usually needed, or wanted, by your audience.

- Add music and anecdotes for more interest.

- Be creative. Add close-ups, distance shots, low angles, and high angles for variety.

- Never apologize for your pictures. If you don't think it's good enough to be in your show, don't include it.

Slideshows have never been easier to create, and people do like them when they're done well.

Working with RAW Files

One of the great debates among advanced digital photographers is whether to use the JPEG or RAW format for recording images. Both formats are capable of producing high-quality pictures, but when you shoot in JPEG mode, the camera processes the image for you so it is complete when you upload it to your computer.

Images captured in RAW format, on the other hand, are not complete when you transfer them to your workstation. This process is more like taking a negative into a darkroom where you can adjust white balance and exposure until you get the perfect image. It's true that you can make those same adjustments in post-production with JPEGs, but it's different because you're readjusting information that's already been set. With RAW you are actually mapping the original bits of information.

One of the battle cries of this book is "good data in; good data out." The better you capture your shot, the easier it will be to produce high-quality output. By shooting in RAW mode, you're able to delay some difficult decisions until you're in the comfort of your own home, working at your computer.

A good example is determining the correct white balance, which is often difficult at the moment of exposure, especially under fluorescent or mixed lighting. When you shoot in JPEG mode you have to make an immediate decision and, if you're wrong, you have to figure out how to correct it later.

In RAW mode, it doesn't make any difference which white balance setting you have when you shoot the picture. The camera just records the "raw" data and lets you fill in the blanks later while at the computer. You can apply different color temperatures to the image, view their appearance, and have the computer apply one that you like without any compromise to image quality. It's just like choosing white balance at the time of exposure (only better, because you're looking at a 17" monitor, not a 2" LCD screen!).

If your camera has the ability to shoot in RAW format, it will include software to work with these images. Photoshop users can also work with RAW files right in Photoshop. Visit the Adobe site (*http://www.adobe.com*) for more information.

No matter which software you use, this method is as close as you can come to a true digital darkroom, and it provides you with maximum flexibility for processing your images. Working with RAW images requires more work and processing time, both at the time of exposure and later at the computer. But for situations in which you want absolute control over quality and final output, RAW is an excellent option.

Which is best for you? A common-sense approach would be to capture at the highest JPEG settings for your "everyday" shooting, and take advantage of the RAW format for difficult lighting situations or when you want to squeeze every drop of quality out of your picture-taking process.

Archive Images for Future Use

Digital images should be treated like any other important computer file: archived and kept in a safe place. Most computers these days have built-in CD-RW drives for burning compact discs, and CDs are an excellent archiving medium. Consider making two sets of archived optical discs for your backup: one set for home, and another to be kept in a remote location—just in case.

When preparing to back up your important photographs, take a few minutes to figure out how you want to organize your files before you start burning CDs. Since digital cameras usually assign names such as *IMG_3298.JPG* to your pictures, you won't be able to go back and find those Paris shots by reading the filenames. Yet, you're probably not going to want to rename each picture individually either.

Instead, give a descriptive name to the folder that contains images of a like kind, such as *Paris Trip 2002*. You can always browse the contents of the folder with an image browser once you're in the general vicinity.

Regardless of which method you embrace, the important thing is to have an orderly system and a regular backup routine. You already know how frustrating it is to look for an old picture buried in a shoebox deep within your closet. Consider digital photography your second chance in life, and take advantage of your computer's ability to store and retrieve information.

Where to Go From Here

Now it's time to shoot. The best thing about digital cameras is that you can take picture after picture without worrying about film-processing costs. And the best way to learn the art and science of photography is to take lots of pictures.

Keep your eyes open, your camera steady, and most importantly: enjoy!

Quick-Reference Tables

Use the following tables as a quick-reference guide for a variety of camera settings. For more detailed explanations for the data listed here, see Chapter 3.

Table 1. Exposure compensation reference guide

Lighting situation	Recommended exposure compensation (via the scale setting)
Subject against a bright sky background (high clouds on sunny day).	Overexpose by 2 (+2.0); use fill flash if within 10 feet
Light object (white color), front lit.	Overexpose by 1.5 (+1.5)
Subject against white sand or snow (e.g., person skiing).	Overexpose by 1.5 (+1.5)
Landscape scene dominated by bright, hazy sky.	Overexpose by 1 (+1.0)
Fair-skinned subjects with bright front lighting.	Overexpose by .5 (+.5)
Subject against green foliage in open sun (e.g., outdoor portrait with background trees and shrubs).	No compensation
Dark-skinned subjects with bright front lighting.	Underexpose by .5 (−.5)
Brightly lit subject against dark background (e.g., theater lighting).	Underexpose by 1 (−1.0)
Dark object (black color), front lit.	Underexpose by 1.5 (−1.5)

Table 2. Flash mode settings

Situation	Recommended flash mode
Outdoor portrait in open shade or sun.	Fill flash (flash forced on)[a]
Subject against bright background, such as hazy sky.	Fill flash (flash forced on)[a]
Wedding and other special events (both indoor and outdoor shooting).	Fill flash (flash forced on)[a]
Subject in brightly lit evening scene such as Times Square, New York, or Sunset Strip, Las Vegas.	Slow synchro flash[a]
Portrait against twilight sky, brightly lit monument, or building.	Slow synchro flash[a]
Portrait in brightly lit room where ambient lighting needs to be preserved.	Slow synchro flash[a]
Subject who typically blinks as flash fires.	Red-eye reduction flash (to eliminate recorded blinking)
Mood portrait by window, bright lamp, or other similar setting.	Flash off (steady camera with tripod or other support)
Sporting event or outdoor concert when shooting from the stands.	Flash off (steady camera with tripod or other support)

[a] On some point-and-shoot cameras, these flash settings are accessible only when you enable manual mode. Cameras typically ship in automatic mode, which limits the number of adjustments that the photographer can change. Refer to your owners manual for more information.

Table 3. White balance settings

Lighting condition	Recommended white balance setting
Sunny, outdoor conditions.	Auto or Daylight
Open shade (e.g., under a tree), indoor portraits by window light, or when flash is on indoors.	Cloudy (add fill flash when possible)
Snow setting, bluish winter light, or when overall light balance is too "cool."	Cloudy
Indoors with flash off and tungsten light is the dominant light source.	Tungsten
Outdoors at sunset or sunrise when light is too "warm."	Tungsten
Indoors when dominant light source is fluorescent tubes.	Fluorescent

Table 4. Camera modes with explanation

Camera mode[a]	Explanation
Programmed Auto (P)	Camera sets both aperture and shutter speed. Good for general photography.
Shutter Priority/Timed Value (TV)	Photographer sets the shutter speed and the camera sets corresponding aperture. Best for action, sports, or running water photography.
Aperture Priority/Aperture Value (AV)	Photographer sets the aperture (f-stop) and the camera sets the corresponding shutter speed. Best for landscape photography or any situation that requires depth-of-field control.
Manual (M)	Photographer sets both aperture and shutter speed. Advanced mode for those with an understanding of photography.
Movie	Camera records short video segments and saves them as a QuickTime, AVI, or MPEG file. Some models also record sound to accompany the video.
Panorama	Camera designates a sequence of shots to be later "stitched together" to create one image with a wide perspective.
Nighttime	Allows for longer shutter speeds (even when the flash is enabled) to enable photography in low ambient light, such as at sunset or for brightly lit interiors. A tripod should be used to help steady the camera when using this mode.

[a] Your camera may have all, some, or only a couple of these modes available. Typically, aperture priority, shutter priority, and manual modes are available only on advanced models.

Table 5. Metering modes with explanation

Metering mode[a]	Explanation
Fvaluative metering	Camera divides viewing area into "segments" and evaluates each area alone and in combination with others. End result is very accurate overall exposure for most scenes. Good choice for general photography.
Spot metering	Camera reads only the center portion of the viewing area, usually within the center brackets or crosshairs. Good choice for situations that require precise exposure control on a particular element in the scene. Most popular use is to correctly meter a person's face in difficult lighting situations.
Center-weighted metering	Reads entire viewfinder area, but with more emphasis placed on central portion of the scene. Typically used for landscape and general photography. Evaluative metering is usually preferred over center weighted.

[a] Many point-and-shoot cameras offer only one metering mode, usually center-weighted or evaluative. Intermediate and advanced models usually include spot metering, too.

Table 6. Exposure starting points for sunset and astrophotography [a]

Subject	ISO speed	Aperture (f-stop)	Shutter speed
Sunset (point at sky without sun shining in viewfinder)	100	Programmed autoexposure	Programmed autoexposure
Full moon	100	f-8	1/250 to 1/500
Quarter moon	100	f-5.6	1/125 to 1/250
Total lunar eclipse	200	f-2.8	2 seconds (use tripod)
Half lunar eclipse	200	f-4	1 second (use tripod)
Auroras borealis	200	f-2.8	2–30 seconds depending on intensity (use tripod)
Star trails	100	f-4	10 minutes or longer (use tripod)
Meteors	100	f-5.6	30 minutes or longer (use tripod)

[a] The settings in Table 6 serve only as starting points for astrophotography. Allow ample time for testing with your equipment and conditions for optimum results.

Table 7. Megapixels to print size reference

Camera type	2MP	3MP	4MP	5MP
Photo quality	5×7	8×10	11×14	12×16
Acceptable	8×10	11×14	12×16	16×20

Table 8. Number of pictures to capacity of memory card reference [a]

	Camera Resolution				
Card Capacity	640 × 480 (.3 MP)	1280 × 960 (1.3 MP)	1600 × 1200 (2 MP)	2048 × 1536 (3.3 MP)	2272 × 1704 (4.1 MP)
8 MB	29	10	7	3	2
16 MB	58	24	14	8	7
32 MB	120	49	30	17	14
64 MB	241	88	61	35	30
128 MB	483	177	123	71	61

[a] The number of pictures listed for each memory card size in this chart is for images saved at the highest quality settings. You can "squeeze" more pictures per card by lowering quality settings, but this is not recommended.

Table 9. Color temperature chart in Kelvin

Degrees Kelvin	Type of light source
1700–1800K	Match flame
1800–2200K	Dawn, dusk, candle flame
2400–2600K	40W incandescent bulb
2800–3000K	100W incandescent bulb
3200–3400K	500W photoflood bulb, Quartz bulbs
4200K	Sun at 20 degree altitude, cool white fluorescent bulb
5400K	Sun at direct noon
5500K	Photographic daylight
5500–6000K	Hazy sun, photo electronic flash, HMI lamp, neons
6500 – 7000K	Bright sun, daylight fluorescent bulb
8000–9000K	Open shade outdoors, overcast sky
9000–10000K	North light, skylight window

Index